G000081116

הסטוריה

The ArtScroll History Series®

Rabbi Nosson Scherman / Rabbi Meir Zlotowitz
General Editors

Daughters

compiled by
Devora Rubin

# of Destiny

Women who revolutionized Jewish life and Torah education

published by

Mesorah Publications, ltd.

FIRST EDITION
First Impression . . . December, 1988
Second Impression . . . January, 1989

Published and Distributed by
MESORAH PUBLICATIONS, Ltd.
Brooklyn, New York 11232

Distributed in Israel by
MESORAH MAFITZIM / J. GROSSMAN
Rechov Harav Uziel 117
Jerusalem, Israel

Distributed in Europe by
J. LEHMANN HEBREW BOOKSELLERS
20 Cambridge Terrace
Gateshead, Tyne and Wear
England NE8 1RP

THE ARTSCROLL HISTORY SERIES®
DAUGHTERS OF DESTINY
© Copyright 1988, by MESORAH PUBLICATIONS, Ltd.
4401 Second Avenue / Brooklyn, N.Y. 11232 / (718) 921-9000

No part of this book may be reproduced
in any form without **written** permission from the copyright holder,
except by a reviewer who wishes to quote brief passages in connection with a review
written for inclusion in magazines or newspapers.

THE RIGHTS OF THE COPYRIGHT HOLDER WILL BE STRICTLY ENFORCED.

ISBN:
0-89906-494-9 (hard cover)
0-89906-495-7 (paperback)

Typography by CompuScribe at ArtScroll Studios, Ltd.
4401 Second Avenue / Brooklyn, N.Y. 11232 / (718) 921-9000

Printed in the United States of America by Noble Book Press Corp.
Bound by Sefercraft, Quality Bookbinders, Ltd. Brooklyn, N.Y.

Foreword

e call it *mesorah* — the means of handing down eternal truths from generation to generation. As Jews, we understand that there is no such thing as the dead past, that history is not an arcane pursuit best left to scholars, that the modern world is not necessarily better educated, better prepared to cope with life's emergencies. Circumstances and perspectives change from generation to generation; *mesorah* is eternal, handed down from parent to child, from teacher to student, from *rebbi* to *talmid*.

Classically, *mesorah* is an oral teaching, and so it is especially appropriate that in this book we chose to speak with our teachers, our *bubbas*, with special women who personify the fine qualities of a true Jewish princess — the *bas melech* who is today such a rarity. Our book attempts to open a window to a world past, which is still very much present today. Through its pages we will plunge into the world of yesterday, a world that accentuated the spiritual and yet retained its essential humanity, with humane traits and characteristics and, yes, human failings as well.

Between World War I and World War II Sarah Schneirer began the Bais Yaakov movement. The experiences of the pioneering students and teachers of those years are quite different from ours — and yet very similar; unique, and yet universal. The life experiences of those who grew up between the two wars, who developed with the Bais Yaakov movement and who experienced personally the devastation of the years of *churban*, may seem removed from our own, and yet they are still timely.

In this spirit we undertook to interview some of those women who were there at that seminal period for Bais Yaakov — as students, as teachers, as wives and daughters of people who were involved in shaping and directing the experiences of the Yeshivah and Bais Yaakov student at that critical time.

And that message which our *bubbas* have to convey to us, the timeless *mesorah* that they have to hand down? A simple one, really: the survival of the nation depends on the Torah. And it is the women, women in public service as teacher or headmistress or Rebbetzin; women, most vitally, as *aishes chayil*, creator of the Jewish home, that will ensure that survival.

Rebbetzin Yehudis Karelitz
Dean of Students
B.Y.A Seminary

Acknowledgments

wo years ago, students of Bais Yaakov Academy were given a project to complete — to write a book. What you are now reading is the result of two years. We would like to extend our appreciation and heartfelt thanks to the many people who made this book possible.

First and foremost are the subjects of our interviews: Rebbetzin Bender, Rebbetzin Feldman, Rebbetzin Ginsburg, Rebbetzin Grunfeld, Rebbetzin Kaplan, Rebbetzin Pincus, Rebbetzin Scheinberg and Rebbetzin Zaks. The hours they gave us and the knowledge we gained cannot be measured. There were times we were shocked, amused, fascinated and educated all in one hour. They made us feel what they felt, learn what they learned, live what they lived. And, in the end, it was their encouragement that enabled us to finish what we started.

We also owe a debt of thanks to Rebbetzin Wiesenfeld, Rebbetzin Benes and Rebbetzin Lubart for their information, time and encouragement. The interesting anecdotes and fascinating pictures from Rebbetzin S. Pernikoff and Mrs. M. Sternberg enhanced our book tremendously.

To understand what this book entailed we must trace it to its roots. The first step was preliminary contact with those whom we wanted to interview. We owe all this to Rebbetzin Y. Karelitz and Rebbetzin S. Ginsburg who made many phone calls and valuable suggestions.

The next step was for girls to go to the houses of these women to conduct the interviews. Chayi Weiss not only went on many interviews, she scheduled them and recruited others to go along.

The list of recruits includes Sara Aliza Reiss, Rena and Shifra Wiesenfeld, Sora Gold, Goldy Gonter, Chani Wulliger, Yehudis Neirenberg and Tzippy Bak. Thanks to you all.

Sometimes the girls took notes of the interviews and other times they recorded them. Tzippy Rosenblatt spent hours transcribing interviews from tapes to make them easier to rewrite.

After the interviews were written into manuscript form, they were given to various girls to be typed and prepared for editing. Mindy Weiss, Kayla Ackerman, Tzippy Rosenblatt, Sora Gold, Mrs. Rubin, Tova Rubin and Mrs. C.E. Pitem spent hours typing. They were assisted by Pearl Frankel, Mindy Berman, Chaya Sora Gross, Galit Bohaddana and Rochel Golombeck, who were there when we needed them.

The typed manuscript was edited by Miriam Stark Zakon whose expertise polished an unfinished work. Her encouragement and helpful advice was invaluable.

Of course, we must thank the various members of B.Y.A.'s great staff. To the Financial Aid Office — thanks for letting us "get in the way." We'll try not to do it anymore. Mrs. Roz Englemeyer and Mrs. E. Goldman, thanks for putting up with us.

A feeling that this project was becoming more of a reality and less of a dream began to emerge when ArtScroll entered the picture. It was a pleasure to come into the office just to talk and discuss things with their wonderful staff. Rabbi Avie Gold was especially helpful in giving his time and attention whenever it was needed.

A special thanks to Mrs. Menucha Silver who waded through mazes of corrections and worked overtime to see this book through. And to Rabbi Nosson Scherman, Rabbi Meir Zlotowitz, Rabbi Shea Brander, Mrs. Faigy Weinbaum, Zissie Glatzer, Bassie Goldstein, Lea Freier, Suri Adler and Faigie Zlotowitz — thanks for everything!

We must inject here a special word of gratitude to our very special teacher Rebbetzin Y. Karelitz. We could not have completed this work without her constant work, support and "push" to see that we were moving.

Finally, thanks to our principals Rabbi Shlomo Teichman and Rabbi Avrohom Greenberg. Their constant support and efforts to see this book through is what made it possible.

Devora Rubin

Table of Contents

Part One

Rebbetzin
Miriam Feldman

> " *Shabbos, which had always been*
> *a welcome break in the week for me,*
> *now became a time of sacrifice ...*
> *On Shabbos we suffered constantly ...*
> *because we refused to work.*
> *I spent those (Shabbos) afternoons*
> *in constant fear ... Any minute I expected*
> *to be caught ... I thanked Hashem*
> *every Shabbos for the miracle*
> *that made me survive that day.* "

Born in the small Polish *shtetl* of Dobara where her father, Rabbi Chaim Lieberman, served as *rav*, Rebbetzin Miriam Feldman spent some time in the Bais Yaakov Seminary in Cracow, until the outbreak of the Second World War forced its closing. With her parents, Rebbetzin Feldman spent most of the war years in a labor camp in the Ural Mountains near Siberia, where with great sacrifice they managed to keep Shabbos and *mitzvos*. Upon their release, they fled to the barren and impoverished area of Bukhara, where she met and wed Rabbi Hirsch Feldman, a *bachur* who had found refuge there as well.

With war's end the family wandered through Poland, Czechoslovakia, and France, establishing a yeshivah wherever they settled. Finally, in 1948, they settled in New York City, and Rabbi Feldman became *mashgiach* in the transplanted Mirrer Yeshiva, where he served until his *petirah* (death).

Today, Rebbetzin Feldman conducts adult education classes in B.Y.A.

Dobara

et me take you to a large village framed by wooded mountains. One can smell the clean fresh air as it quietly makes waves in the shimmering blue rivers that speckle the town. It is quite obviously an agricultural village with quaint farms surrounded by blossoming vegetation.

Dobara is rather a large village but quite tiny as far as towns go. Compared to Cracow, a short distance away, Dobara is not even worthy of mention. Yet, it is important to me for this was the town where my father was *rav*, the town in which I was born.

We lived in our own house surrounded by proofs of country living. On one side was a vegetable garden with tomatoes, cucumbers, potatoes and whatnot. On the other side was our flower garden. Shavuos time, when all was in bloom, the beauty of the blossoms framed by the woody background was a sight to behold.

The residents of the city were mostly non-Jewish farmers. My father was the *rav* of the one *shul* we had, thus the *rav* of the town. All of the Jews of the village were united under his leadership but we were a small group with little voice or power.

In Dobara, there were no Bais Yaakov schools. The school I attended was a public school filled with Polish pupils. There were a few other religious girls in my class and we kept to ourselves as much as possible. The administration and teaching staff consisted only of Polish anti-Semites. Although we were by far the best students, we were treated the worst because of our beliefs. Our classwork was never appreciated and they were always looking for ways to prove to themselves that we were bad and they were better. As usual, for *Yidden* in *galus* (exile) we became the scapegoats for any mishap.

The anti-Semitism of the Polish people is among the strongest of any nation. Until today I have an inherent fear of any non-Jew because of the hatred I witnessed daily. It was a tradition of theirs, passed on from parents to child, from generation to generation. In school our Polish classmates took the lunches our mothers prepared for us with so much love and care and they ate the stolen food right in front of our faces. They looked at us with malice and superiority, knowing that no one would punish them. The teachers turned their backs on such incidents and their silence encouraged more "accidents" and lost lunches. We were powerless to do anything and the

Polish children reveled at their ability to lord over us. Such daily occurrences can make a profound impression on a child. This fear of *goyim* (gentiles) is so much a part of me that whenever I see a gentile in the street today and he doesn't come over to slap me, I thank *Hakadosh Baruch Hu* (G-d).

☙ ☙ ☙

The level of religious feelings then, it seems to me, was much deeper than today.

For example, *Tishah B'Av* was not merely a day when we abstained from eating. The tragedy of the *churban* (destruction of the Temple) was actually felt. At night, the neighborhood women assembled at my house carrying pots or low stools to sit on. Each held a small *Megillas Eichah*. As my mother read aloud of the destruction of our *Beis Hamikdash* (Temple), tears poured down the faces of these sweet, simple *Yiddishe mammas*. Although some might not even have known what the words meant, the intense feelings that permeated the room pierced our hearts.

I was a young child and did not really understand what was going on, but the anguish and sadness they felt remains impressed in my mind until today.

When *Elul* came around, my father was in a world of his own, totally removed from the daily routine. No one could talk to him about anything because his mind was occupied only by the spiritual preparations for the *Yomim Noraim* (days of awe). My mother understood this and would not approach my father for anything, even to pay necessary expenses. He did not carry money or change around with him during this month.

Everyone had an unbelievable fear of *Elul* and the Day of Judgment. We felt it in the air, in the streets, in the stores; these feelings called for quiet introspection in order to improve one's ways. My father would come home after *Shacharis* (morning prayers) with his *bekeshe* (shirt) and other clothes soaking wet from his tears.

On Yom Kippur itself, women and men dressed in white, creating the illusion of heavenly beings. My mother wore a starched white dress covered by a white apron. It was a tradition in my family that women wear these aprons as men do their *tzitzis* — as a type of *shemirah* (protection). Throughout our travels my mother kept her apron with her and I still have it today. I can picture her in my mind, dressed in pure white, pouring her heart out to the *Ribbono Shel*

Olam (Master of the universe), the tears streaming down her face. By the end of the day we felt cleansed and closer to *Hashem* (G-d).

Our year revolved around these holy interludes and often we'd prepare many months ahead in anticipation.

A perfect illustration of this was the festival of Pesach. We had no ready-to-eat food products or special food packaged to be "Kosher for Pesach." Everything we needed we had to prepare from scratch, using what we had available when it was in season. Consequently we planned for Pesach as early as Chanukah time. Chanukah time was the "geese season," when these fowl were relatively cheap and obtainable. One year the birds came into market earlier than usual, and we cared for and raised these geese for several months until they reached maturity. Right before Chanukah we took the geese we bought or raised to the *shochet* (butcher) for slaughter. For a small fee he slaughtered the fowl and we took them home to begin the long job of using them to reap maximum benefit.

First, we removed the feathers, saving each precious one to use as down stuffing. These feathers would be used to fill quilt covers and pillows which would eventually be given as wedding presents to a young couple. These bedcovers were essential to combat the bitter cold of the Polish winter.

The plucked poultry then had to be *kashered* according to *halachah* (Jewish law) before we could use any of their parts for food. We ate the meat during Chanukah and several weeks afterwards, until we exhausted our supply. The fat from the geese was melted over a flame to be used as *schmaltz* for Pesach.

When Pesach finally arrived our hardest job began — cleaning the meat. Each family had its own well, so everyone could use as much water as they needed. Drawing the water was a difficult task and every drop of water had to be strained through a large white sheet to filter out the bugs. Only then could this water be used to *kasher* the large amounts of meat we needed for *Yom Tov* (holiday).

We even made our own ground coffee from raw coffee beans. My mother bought the coffee plant, the shells still intact. She roasted the beans until they were brown and then finely chopped them in a special grinder called a *mershzer*. Pepper was also ground in the same time consuming manner until it became a very fine powder.

Cleaning for Pesach was tediously hard work. We had to go out to the well to draw the water we needed for every job, big or small.

All the work was that much harder and required that much more effort.

We spent so many months planning for *Yom Tov* and so much time preparing and working, that when Pesach actually came we really felt a feeling of *cherus* (freedom). The work and effort that went into Pesach preparations really added to the joy of the holiday. We felt everything was worth the peace and serenity of the holiday.

I remember the *seder* night in my home. My father sat at the head of the table, straight and tall, like a king addressing his subjects. My mother sat opposite, her radiant face framed by the white turban-like head covering, a *shterentichel*. This she wore as a queen wears her crown. Having the entire family close together made the joy even greater. My father's chassidic background was apparent in the way he conducted the *seder*. His beautiful songs added spice and flavor to the fascinating retelling of the *Haggadah*.

❦ ❦ ❦

We lived in Dobara until I was twelve years old. That year my sister became engaged to a young scholar named Rabbi Avraham Englard. The excitement in the air was tangible; the *rav's* daughter was getting married! It was understood that everyone in town was invited and all wanted to pitch in and help. For two weeks prior to the *chassunah* (wedding) we hired a cook to help my mother. The village women began to send over food, trays of pastries and cakes, delicious smells wafting through the air . As the food entered the house, the furniture departed. Every extraneous piece was moved into storage to make room for the many people expected.

The day of the *chassunah* arrived. We all dressed in our Shabbos best and gathered at the *shul*. The Poles stopped their work to watch the spectacle — masses of Jews singing and dancing in joyous exultation. After the *chupah* (ceremony) everyone slowly gravitated towards our house to partake of the *seudas mitzvah* (wedding feast). The singing, dancing and speeches extended well into the night.

Several days later my family and I left the city. My father had transferred his *rabbonus* to his new son-in-law and accepted a position in a *shul* in the city of Sanz. Although life in Dobara was quiet and pleasant, the Jewish community was small. My parents wanted to go to a place where there would be proper schools for us children and Sanz seemed to be the answer.

Sanz

icture a large bustling city, wooded forests on the outskirts, fresh-water rivers flowing through grassy fields, all this framed by the impressive Alps. This was Sanz. With a population of approximately fifty thousand, Sanz was a tremendous change from quaint little Dobara.

There were many adjustments that came with our move. Instead of having our own house and gardens as we did in Dobara, we lived in a small rented apartment. There were many *shuls* and *shteiblach* throughout the city but there was no *rav* of the town whose leadership was supreme. My father joined the ranks of the other *rabbanim* of the town, leading his congregants.

His congregants, and most of the other Jews in the neighborhood, made their livelihoods in various ways. They could not be doctors, lawyers, or other professionals because Polish colleges were closed to Jews. The educated gentiles in town had monopolies over those professions. Jews had to be content being the shoemakers, tailors, and other types of craftsmen. Some of the richer members of the *kehillah* (community) made their money through business. The most flourishing of these was the lumber business. They would hire the lower class Poles to chop from the seemingly endless forests. This lumber was sold all over the country, and made, all in all, a profitable business.

All these Jews formed factions among themselves, *davening* (praying) in their own *shuls*, living within their levels of *Yiddishkeit*. There were the very learned *Chassidim*, the *frum* (observant) but unlearned simple Jews, *talmidei chachamim* (scholars) who worked a half a day and learned the other half. Then there were other Jews who followed the doctrines of the Haskalah, "adapting" *Yiddishkeit* to the times. Others became Communists and Bundists, often becoming totally irreligious. The Zionist groups, who had turned their Jewish religion into a love of a land instead of a love of *Hashem*, were very powerful.

❦ ❦ ❦

Our lives were truly Torah centered. In Hebrew we do not have specific names for the days of the week as do other languages. Instead we say, "the first day to Shabbos," "the second day to Shabbos," and so on. This is because a Jew is supposed to center his life around Shabbos, spending each day in preparation and anticipation of Shabbos.

We looked forward to Shabbos the whole week as a form of retreat. During the week we actually felt *galus* in our bones through the hate the non-Jews constantly exhibited. It made us appreciate a day of sanctity and peace so much more. Each of the three meals was very special, characterized by lively and spirited singing.

For me, however, Shabbos was partly a *nisayon* (test). There were very few opportunities open to Jews in Poland. Because of the strong anti-Semitic feelings, colleges and, consequently, professions were closed to Jews. Many smart youths were frustrated at the prospect of a dim and poor future. This led to a strong desire to emigrate to Israel. They hoped that there they could live peacefully without the hate and prejudice of Poland. Zionist groups had strong influences over those who felt a "homeland" would solve their problems. Many young Jewish boys and girls, including those from very fine Jewish homes, joined these groups. They would form a *hachshara* where young people would get together to prepare for *aliya*, going up to Israel. By learning how to farm and care for domestic animals, they felt that they would be ready to move to Israel, a country that was underdeveloped agriculturally.

Their desires, however, were not so easily fulfilled. Palestine, as Israel was known then, was under British mandate and the English government made it very difficult for Jews to get passes to Israel. These Zionist groups remained large because they could not emigrate and therefore their membership did not decrease. On Shabbos they would get together to talk about their dreams and plans to go to Palestine, their ultimate goal. They sang songs, socialized and just had a good time. I felt torn between going along with my friends, who were members, or staying home alone in the company of my family. These friends told me of the wonderful times they had and encouraged me to join their meetings. Somehow my parents' influence triumphed for I just could not go to such gatherings. Boys and girls joined together in these groups and the whole atmosphere was unacceptable to me. Therefore, most of my Shabbos afternoons were spent quietly at home enjoying the sense of peace that Shabbos always brings.

❧ ❧ ❧

During the week, I attended public school where I learned secular subjects. After lunch I went to Bais Yaakov, one of the many new schools established by students of Sarah Schneirer. There we learned subjects such as *Chumash*, *Navi*, Jewish History, etc. For the first time in my life I was going to a religious school with Jewish girls of my own age. It was so exciting to have this fabulous opportunity. The staff of teachers were mainly graduates of the Bais Yaakov Seminary of Cracow, young, intelligent and capable girls from whom we learned a tremendous amount.

As I got older Bnos groups were formed to, in a sense, combat the influence of the irreligious groups in the area. Bnos was my salvation. The organization grew to include about five hundred girls. We would get together about two o'clock in the afternoon and stay until after Shabbos. Amidst the fun and laughter, one powerful lesson was learned: We saw that *frum* girls can have fun within the realm of Torah, and that we did not need the irreligious youth groups. After the *divrei Torah* (words of Torah) were said, the games were played, and the songs sung, we ate *Shalosh Seudos* (the third Shabbos meal) and went home.

When summer came around, we all packed up and went to a village in the mountains. In eager anticipation, we threw our valises into the back of the wagon and jumped in after them. The bumpety-bump of the rickety wheels on the rocky dirt road was music to our ears.

We arrived at the rented houses that were going to be home for the next couple of weeks. About fifty sixteen-year-old girls made their way through the houses, *shlepping* valises, airing out beds and opening the windows. Each girl was assigned a different day to cook for her apartment. Everyone took care of their own sleeping space and belongings.

Our days were filled with fascinating *shiurim* (classes), canoeing in the vast river, exploring the beautiful countryside, rolling down grassy slopes, laughter and singing. We could not get enough of it and, when it was time to go home, everyone bade good-bye reluctantly, wistfully.

Bais Yaakov

s I got older, I saw how difficult it was for my parents to make ends meet. I already had graduated high school and wanted to learn some kind of trade to earn money. My parents were appalled at the thought that the daughter of a *rav* learn a trade. Preposterous! However, they realized that I needed some type of outlet and, in 1938, sent me to study at Bais Yaakov Seminary of Cracow. This was a tremendous sacrifice for them emotionally and monetarily. I, who had never been away from home before, was leaving for two years. Furthermore, tuition was fifty *zlotys*, an enormous amount of money, and there was still the expense of the journey to Cracow to consider. Nevertheless, my parents overcame these difficulties and sent me to Bais Yaakov.

I arrived there after the death of Sarah Schneirer. The one who took over where Sarah Schneirer left off was Rebbetzin Biegun. She was an unusual woman: bright, charismatic, with a strong influence on all those she encountered. She understood that her position entailed the responsibility of molding the future mothers of *Klal Yisrael* and therefore was uncompromising when it came to a question of *chinuch* (education). Rebbetzin Biegun demanded one hundred percent from all her girls and yet was loved by each and every one.

She came to Bais Yaakov as a student; Chana Grossfeld was her maiden name. She rose to become one of Sarah Schneirer's most prized pupils and trusted lieutenants. Several years later, she married R' Yossi Biegun, a young *talmid chacham* from Mirrer Yeshiva. After the death of Sarah Schneirer, Rebbetzin Biegun carried on her work. Her life was the school. She taught classes, made school policies and watched the progress of each and every girl. She instilled in me a lifelong lesson: that every Jewess should be proud of her heritage. A *bas Yisrael* (Jewish girl) should never want to melt into the *goyishe* world — she should walk with her back straight, her head held high, proud of her *Yiddishkeit*. This lesson eventually carried me through many years of *nisyonos*.

The study in Cracow was intensive. Within a short span of time, we were expected to cover a lot of ground and by working hard we were able to live up to those expectations. My classmates were all exceptional students, many from very fine homes. One girl who comes to my mind is Sarah Kotler [Rebbetzin Schwartzman — Ed.]. She was the daughter of R' Aharon Kotler and although she graduated soon after I came, leaving me little time to get to know her better, she made a profound impression on me. She was a brilliant girl, a true *baalas middos* (one posessing fine character traits), a student we newcomers looked up to.

What I really liked best about Cracow was the opportunity to live and learn with religious girls of different and varied backgrounds. I made friends from Germany, France and all parts of Poland. We were all united because of Bais Yaakov. It was an ideal situation that enabled us to gain a tremendous amount of knowledge in the prime years of our development while still living in a sheltered environment.

The holidays there were wonderful and Shabbos was a weekly treat. Friday night we gathered together in the large dining room to eat the Shabbos meal, teachers and students celebrating in harmony. We sang between courses with liveliness and excitement. After we finished eating, we cleaned the tables and pushed them aside. In the space we cleared, we joined hands and danced together, singing as our feet pounded the floors. *Shalosh Seudos* was even more special. Although the candles had long since burned out, we created a brightness of our own. Sitting close together in the dark dining room we ate and sang, enjoying the peace and holiness of Shabbos.

❧ ❧ ❧

The summer of 1939 brought us to our camp in the mountains. Life went on as usual for us students as we experienced all the fun, sunshine and learning of the past years. Because we had absolutely no contact with the outside world, we had no idea of the war situation. Radios and newspapers were non-existent in our little haven up in the country. Our first hint of the imminence of war was when an American girl received a letter from the American ambassador telling her to leave Poland as soon as possible. The letter informed her that war had already erupted in Europe. She was to leave as soon as possible, for the longer she remained in Poland the more danger she would find herself in. Panic erupted, disturbing the peace of camp. No one knew what to expect. Most of us could not recollect World War I and we had no idea how this would affect our lives. The entire camp was a beehive of unrest.

The administration ended the summer sessions early that year and most of the girls returned home to their families as soon as possible. I said goodbye to my friends, many of whom I'd never see again, and took a bus back to Sanz. The windows of the bus were covered with black paper to avoid any glare from the windows and keep it from being spotted. We traveled at night because the bombings had already started and it is hard to bomb a moving vehicle in darkness. *Baruch Hashem* (thank G-d) we arrived home safely.

The Journey Begins

hen I returned to Sanz I found the town in an uproar. No one knew what to do or where to go. My family decided to move to the city of Lvov (Lemberg), where my grandmother lived. This city had just been annexed by Russia according to the terms of the Von Ribbentrop-Molotov Agreement [see Rebbetzin Ginsburg's interview — Ed.]. A city under Russian jurisdiction seemed safer than a Polish city that might soon be under German occupation.

Many of the men ran away because, they reasoned, they might be taken into captivity or drafted into the army. Women, on the other hand, are usually left alone. Since most people did not expect the war to last long, the husbands went to "safe" cities, leaving their wives behind, confident that they would soon return. My brother-in-law was in Lvov and so I went to Dobara to help my sister.

For a long time my sister, her two children and I were left without contact with the rest of the family. We felt alone, lost and unsafe. After a while, a distant relative came to give us money and urge us to leave before the Germans came and made leaving impossible. We hired a Pole to take us over the border, to the San river, and escort us across to the other side. The whole trip was illegal and had to be done with the utmost secrecy.

Darkness engulfed us, me and my sister, as we went to the forest to meet with the Pole. Each of us held a child and as many packages as we could carry. The night was pitch black and stormy as we stalked the forest with our big burly guide. We were terrified every step of the way for, even if no German patrol caught us, the Pole had us at his mercy. He could have done almost anything he wanted to us because we would never be able to report him anyway. *Baruch Hashem* we arrived at the river safely.

He then told us that instead of the price agreed upon he wanted all our money. What could we do? He could take all our money and not row us across anyway and we so desperately needed to cross the border. Suddenly the baby cried. Try as we did to keep him quiet, the crying was heard. A German officer approached us and demanded to know what our business there was. On the verge of tears, my sister stammered out how her husband was in the army and, what did he want of two helpless girls and children? Out of the "kindness of his heart" he took our jewelry and left us alone. The Pole was then "nice" enough to row us across the river in exchange for the rest of our money. However, when we were on the other side, instead of taking us to the city as he was supposed to, he left us on the bank of the river and went on his way.

It was the dead of night, we had two small children, and absolutely no money to speak of. There was no way for us to know in what direction to walk to reach the city. My sister spotted a light in the distance and decided to investigate where it was coming from. She carried one of the children while I stayed with the other. Five minutes, ten minutes, twenty minutes went by, but my sister had not yet returned. I felt totally alone and afraid. Time passed as I waited with nervous impatience. Suddenly I heard a rustling behind me. I whirled around with a mixture of fear and hope, to find a rough-looking Polish peasant in back of me. Gasping in fright I bolted, clutching the child to me.

"Don't be scared," said the burly Pole. "Your sister is in the house and she sent me here to meet you. Your must walk very carefully, on the balls of your feet, so as not to make any noisy rustling sounds. If a Russian officer catches us without the proper papers, you and I will be arrested as spies." Stealthily we walked, I carrying the baby and he leading the way, until we reached his home. I sighed with joy and relief when I saw my sister and her child sitting there peacefully. That night we slept on the hard wooden floor in the front room of the house with one blanket to drive away the cold.

The next morning we thanked our host and went into the city. Interestingly enough, it was the small city of Chelm, the setting of many fables and stories. We, however, were in a serious mood, looking for a way to get to Lvov. As we approached the center of town we saw many Jewish refugees also trying to escape to Lvov. Everyone gathered together, pooled funds and hired a wagon and driver to go to Lvov. With obvious *hashgachah pratis* (divine intervention) we arrived there safely and were happily reunited with our family.

❦ ❦ ❦

Being in Lvov was a relief to us for not only were we temporarily out of danger, we could now gain strength from the rest of our family. However, life itself was difficult and unsettling. There was absolutely no Jewish business because all free enterprise was illegal under the communist system. When Russia took over Poland, they milked the cities of their resources and sent all available food and clothes to Russia. The only way to obtain these necessities was to barter goods such as towels or soap on the black market in exchange for food. This was how we survived from day to day.

Shortly after our arrival we were faced with a dilemma. The Russian government who now occupied Lvov "requested" that we accept their "generous" offer of Russian citizenship. We had the choice of becoming citizens of Russia or retaining our Polish identity in hope of someday returning. Although we knew that, as of now, Poland had no status as a country, we were more afraid of Communist Russia than the lack of a homeland. Therefore we decided not to be Russian citizens but to remain citizens of Poland in exile. That Shabbos, the K.G.B., then known as the NKVD, came to town and "paid us a visit." They accused us of committing a crime against the beloved mother country by not accepting Russian citizenship. We were all put under immediate arrest.

Residents of Lvov became Russian citizens automatically when the Russians occupied the city. They came out of their houses, dressed in their Shabbos best, and watched in horror as we were led into trucks. Our neighbors ran back inside, emerging minutes later with *challos*, chickens and other food to give us. They pushed the packages of food into our arms, throwing loaves of bread to us as the truck began to move away. Helplessly, they watched, knowing that we were going to a place from where few returned.

At the time it seemed that we made the wrong choice and had just jeopardized our lives. Some Jews became Russian citizens and were left alone, apparently safe. Others had hidden when the Russians first approached us. My sister's in-laws hid in a basement together with my nephew, the baby I took care of on the trip from Dobara to Lvov. Our one consolation was the feeling that they were safe. It was only several years later that we learned that we had been saved and not they. We went through two years of hard labor but, *Baruch Hashem*, many of us survived, while the Jews of Lvov, my relatives included, perished when the Germans occupied the city.

❦   ❦   ❦

We were allowed to take as many possessions as we could carry. What we had in our hands was all that we owned in the world. The

Russian officers brutally pulled us forward, dragging us as they went and pushing us into the long train ahead. These were boxcar-like trains, and they packed as many people as possible in the small compartments. Many men, women, and children were pushed into cars that were meant for one or two passengers.

The trip seemed endless, miles and miles of empty wilderness were passed. Every day the soldiers came into the cars and counted us to make sure no one ran away. There were no toilets on the train. Every so often we were all led under the tracks to relieve ourselves. The embarrassment and lack of dignity we suffered were worse that the physical hardships to come.

We were given one hot meal each day, nourishing beef soup — one hundred percent unkosher. Being that there was nothing else, we existed on the hard stale bread they gave us. Sometimes we received a treat, plain hot water. We dipped our bread into the water, making it soft and tasty. This concoction, *kipyatok* as it was called, was considered a delicacy to be looked forward to.

Traveling with us were Jews from all types of backgrounds, *frum* and non-*frum* alike. Every day my father made a *minyan* (group of ten men) for *davening* and made sure to put on *tefillin* although this was against the orders of the Russians. The trip was marked by a widespread sense of hopelessness. Through the tiny windows we saw endless land. As the wheels turned bringing us further and further into Russia, our faces mirrored our fears. Where were we going?

Russian Prison Camp

e arrived in a labor camp in a part of Russia known as the Ural Mountains. It was an area near Siberia and quite similar in climate. The endless forests were almost always freezing cold although the air was fresh and healthy. This camp was far from any active battlefields and we were uninvolved in the war, ignorant of what was going on outside.

We were sent to live in relatively pleasant prison barracks. The wooden room was spacious, with beds for all its occupants. Nevertheless the freezing cold was still difficult to combat. While indoors, we had a large iron oven for cooking and heat. There were plenty of trees around from which we cut firewood in our spare time. We had no electricity or candles, only a kerosene lamp that gave off a very dim spark. Sometimes, when we were unable to get kerosene, I would huddle to the fire as close as I could, straining to see the words of a letter or a book.

This labor camp was mainly for political prisoners or small time offenders against the Russian government. We lived among the other inmates in the barracks but, *Baruch Hashem*, my family was kept together and we could be a source of comfort to each other. Some families were torn apart, wives separated from their husbands, children from parents.

❀　❀　❀

My sister's husband was determined not to work on Shabbos. He claimed to be sick, hoping to be given the day to recover. He was taken to the best Russian doctors to find out the nature of his "illness." The doctors reported him to be in perfect health and promptly sent him back to work. The Russians, who dislike being crossed, decided not to send him back to have it "easy" working alongside his family. Instead, he was separated from his wife and sent to work with other single men. Shortly thereafter he burned his foot with hot water and was sent to the hospital. This time the injury was authentic and he was relieved of that extremely hard labor. The pain of his wound was a blessing from *Hashem* for, had he been subjected to the labor he had been doing throughout our stay, he might not have survived. Now he could also be together with his family.

Throughout our stay I was close to my family, especially my father. He brought along a *Chumash* and a *Mishnayos* wherever we went. Although he was an elderly man and often weak, he always took time out to teach me when he could have been resting. He would show me the *mishnah* in *Pirkei Avos* and patiently explain the lessons to be learned. My brother-in-law was also a source of courage to me. His sacrifice to keep *Yiddishkeit* alive in a place so far removed from Torah helped keep us going.

The Torah leadership within the labor camp was a group of Polish *chassidim* that included my father and brother-in-law. Every morning, although they had a long day ahead, they got up early to *daven Shacharis* with a *minyan*. They kept up our will to live, our faith that *Hakadosh Baruch Hu* wouldn't forsake us. We kept His commandments as best as we could and had trust in His Providence.

❧ ❧ ❧

Day-to-day living was very difficult. It was still dark as night when we awoke. We were divided into work groups of several men and one woman. Each day we trooped into the woods, prepared to spend the next fourteen hours doing hard labor.

Everyone — unless, like my parents, they were physically ill or elderly — worked from morning until night. Our camp was situated in a vast tundra. There seemed to be only trees covered with green moss for as far as the eye could see. Our job was to chop down large trees and then shear away the branches, leaving a smooth log. These logs were sent to the army to be used in the construction of boats, ships and airplanes.

Chopping trees is a very dangerous occupation. Carelessness could cause injuries or fatalities to many people. We were taught to first examine the tree to try and judge in what direction it would fall when chopped down. Each of us had an ax to continuously hit the bottom of the tree. Sometimes, as we were working, the tree would become uprooted — a dangerous situation. If we did not run away in time we would not only be drenched by the mud but we could also get hurt. After the trees were felled we had to further cut the wood into pieces of a more convenient size for the Russians to use.

We received our share of food according to how well we worked. Anyone whose work was considered below the level of his capabilities was judged to be an enemy of the regime. Often camp officers withheld one's food for not completing the work quota. Thank G-d I was young, energetic and able to work well, and therefore always received my rightful share.

When we had left Lvov, we took along merchandise to barter for food. Besides the bare essentials we took towels, sheets and bars of soap. Rubles were practically valueless, while these commodities could be traded for food. The Russians who admitted us to the camp did not confiscate these goods and we were able to use them throughout our stay. For a piece of soap we could get potatoes, butter or cheese. However, kosher meat was unobtainable and during our entire exile we never tasted meat.

We were not allowed to return home for lunch but, at twelve o'clock every day, we were served on the job. The camp kitchen would send steaming hot dishes of food to the freezing, hungry laborers. Each prisoner's name was called out and, if they had money to pay, they received a portion of food. The meals they served were mouth-watering dishes such as hot meat goulash . . . which was not kosher. During lunchtime my brother, Alter, used to go to the river near his work area to fish. My mother cooked this fish over the stove and each day she gave me a fish sandwich to take to work. When lunch was sold to the rest of the workers I had my sandwich to eat. By the time twelve o'clock came around, my bread and fish sandwich was frozen solid. I had to place it on a rack over the fire in order to heat it so that it was soft enough to eat. Only a few other prisoners kept kosher and we often felt pangs of envy when the other prisoners ate their delicious, nourishing, hot food and we had only our barely thawed-out sandwiches.

This noon hour was our only break of the day. At this time the good workers were rewarded for their efforts. All the *stachanovkas*, outstanding workers, would get their food ration for the day and the option to buy their reward. Some days we were offered *fafaikas*, warm, quilted jackets. Other days they sold *valikes*, sheepskin-lined boots to help us combat the cold. The cost was minimal. However, one had to be eligible to buy the food and clothes by completing one's work quota, by being a *stachanovka*.

Everyone sat around eating lunch, warming their bodies and smoking tobacco rolled up in old newspapers.

After a while we became accustomed to the harsh labor and it got easier. The cold climate killed many of the harmful germs and the mountain air was healthy. The worst part was the difficult schedule, almost constant work from day until night. I usually returned home to the barracks totally exhausted. Although it was early in the evening, it was as dark as midnight. I tumbled into bed as soon as I got home.

❀   ❀   ❀

Shabbos brought a special problem. My father used to tie my sandwich around my neck. In this way, I was able to avoid carrying on Shabbos. However, even though I now had my lunch I could not heat it up. I had to eat it the way it was, usually frozen. Shabbos, which had always been a welcome break in the week for me, now became a time of sacrifice. Usually we kept warm by constantly moving while working, then reviving ourselves with the warm food. On Shabbos we suffered constantly, not only

existed. For the past two years the life of a prisoner was the only life we knew. Yet, before our eyes sat a mother feeding a child, a small girl dressed properly with a little bow in her hair, a young boy sucking a lollipop as he gazed out the window. The scene was overwhelming.

They in turn saw us, two bedraggled youngsters clutching two loaves of bread as if they were gold.

"... What are two young children doing on your own... where are your parents ... look how tired and pale they are ... would you like a bite to eat? ... Peter, move over and let the boy sit ... bring me that blanket, Natasha, the girl looks cold ..."

Unable to deal with the situation any longer, I burst into tears, explaining all that happened. They listened with sympathy as they pressed food into our hands. Some of these people were Jewish and some were not. All of them were being evacuated from the outskirts of Russia deeper into the country where the government hoped they would be safe from the war. They comforted us, reassuring us that we would soon be reunited with our families.

Several hours and two trains later, we caught up with our families. My parents were literally crying with joy. They too had stopped at every station to look if we had somehow arrived there. Now we were together again.

As we progressed, we saw signposts along the way with the names of the cities we were going through. We began to feel that the idea of illegally crossing the border was too dangerous to attempt. My family and I began to discuss alternate plans, each contributing ideas. One thing we all agreed upon was finding a place with a warmer climate after the bitter Russian winters we had been subjected to. We scanned the city signposts, unsure where to get off or what place would have the best opportunities for us.

We were approaching Tashkent, a state in Russia known to have a warm climate. It was part of the region called Uzbekistan where the Uzbek, an Arab-like people, lived.

Bukhara was a city within this state. Through several old *sefarim* (books) my father learned that some generations ago a Jewish community had been established there. He was weak and not feeling well at the time. Therefore, he felt the first priority was to find a place with a Jewish burial ground. Since Bukhara did have a record of a Jewish community, they would probably have one. Furthermore, my father had once heard of a specific *rav* living there. Everything considered, we decided to temporarily settle in Bukhara.

Altogether, the trip took several weeks. We traveled the width of Russia, passing through its most scenic countryside. The Volga, the biggest river in Russia, is absolutely beautiful. Russia is a country rich in natural resources and land, but their government ruined and wasted it all. However much we enjoyed the scenery, the trip was long and tiring and we were relieved when it was finally over.

Bukhara

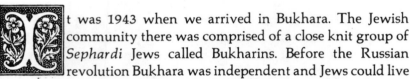It was 1943 when we arrived in Bukhara. The Jewish community there was comprised of a close knit group of *Sephardi* Jews called Bukharins. Before the Russian revolution Bukhara was independent and Jews could live in peace. Several *gedolim* (sages) founded this settlement and spread Torah in the surrounding areas. My father found many ancient, valuable *sefarim* there written by famous *gedolim* testifying to the fact that the previous generation must have had many learned scholars. During the Revolution many of these *rabbanim* were killed and *shuls* burned, the community left desolate. Most of the Jews who were left were the illiterate, unlearned lower class, immersed in the surrounding society. We could barely tell the difference between Jews and *goyim*. There was absolutely nothing distinctively or inherently Jewish about them. The entire spirit of the community lacked *Yiddishkeit*. There were no *yeshivos* to educate the younger generation and maybe it was due to this that their proud heritage had so deteriorated. They only religiously kept some basic *mitzvos* such as Shabbos and the laws of family purity.

Shortly after our arrival, my father found the remnants of the rich Jewish community that had been destroyed during the Russian revolution. The *shuls* that had survived were beautifully constructed, obviously belonging to a wealthy class. Only one of these *shuls* was actually in use. There, my father encountered a few learned people, *mekubalim* (kabbalists) in fact. They sat together in the manner of other Bukharins, crosslegged on the floor like Arabs. They had no chairs or normal tables but either sat directly on the floor or slightly elevated on rocks around low circular tables. We could not go to their *shuls* to *daven* because their *minhagim*

(traditions) were very different from ours.

We *Ashkenazim* got together in a separate room and organized a *minyan* there for the men. The girls had to *daven* on their own at home.

In Bukhara, we were fortunate to join with a leader of Jewry, a *talmid chacham*. The Tshebiner *Rav*, Rabbi Weidenfeld, was also trying to escape war torn Europe and had come to Bukhara en route to *Eretz Yisrael*. Wherever he went, the *Yidden* he was among relied on him to lead and guide them. We clung to him, asking him the myriad of *halachic* questions that came up. He was a leading Torah authority of the time.

❀   ❀   ❀

Upon arrival we knew no one and had no place to stay. Tired and worn out from the journey, we went from house to house asking people for lodging. At first doors were slammed in our faces by the Jewish residents who were suspicious of us. However, when they glimpsed my father in the background they realized we were *frum* *Yidden*. His long beard and distinguished appearance earned him the title of *Chacham* (wise man).

These simple people let us inside and gave us temporary shelter. We were given one room, with only the floor to sleep on. For the next couple of years we lived in a one-room, dirt-floor apartment, with no sink or toilet. A tiny oven in the corner was our only "convenience." These accommodations were even worse than where we had lived during our years in the Russian labor camp.

My parents, my sister with her husband and child, my brother and I were together. Our "house" was hard to keep clean with so many people living there. We had no beds or mattresses and had to sleep on the hard filthy floor. We had no water with which to clean ourselves or our house. To get even the miminal amount needed to live we had to go to the far-away well and *shlep* it. The hot climate and dirty environment was healthy for the lice, making them multiply by the thousands. The lice were carriers of the typhus virus, generously giving it to many of us. Lice also feed on human blood, causing many people to suffer from anemia.

As we came to know the Bukharins we found them hospitable and friendly. However, there were obvious differences between us and them. Their physical appearance was foreign, exotic in its own way. They were very good looking, with nice dark complexions, white teeth and gorgeous oriental eyes. We looked pale and inconspicuous in comparison.

The differences were much more than just physical. We spoke Russian and Yiddish, while they spoke only an Arabic dialect called Bukharin (although a few knew Hebrew). The language barrier made it very difficult for us to communicate with them. They were suspicious of us not only because we were conspicuously foreign and spoke a different language, but because of our *Yiddishkeit* as well. Because there were no *gedolim* and they had virtually no connection with larger Jewish communities, the Bukharins had no official calendar. We had a proper calendar and knew all the *zemanim* (proper times). Consequently, we knew to start Shabbos shortly before sunset, while they started Shabbos a full hour before. This was one *mitzvah* they tried to keep and they looked upon us as *goyim* because we started Shabbos later than them.

Because of our differences they were unsure as to whether we were friend or foe. After several years of living among them they saw that we were on their side. We, too, hated the government and considered them our enemies. With our newly established rapport we tried to start doing business with them. However, every venture was done on a very small scale because of the danger involved. Anyone caught committing any small offense would be sentenced from five to ten years in prison. We often heard of people who were caught operating illegal businesses and immediately put into jail. Countless times collections were set up to raise money to secure the release of a Jew in captivity. Although we never had enough for ourselves, everyone always scraped off at least a few pennies for *pidyon shevuyim* (saving a Jewish life).

❦ ❦ ❦

We had come to Bukhara in the hope of living in a warm climate after the bitter cold we lived through. We weren't prepared for the unbearable heat we encountered. One could practically fry an egg on the street. In addition to the uncomfortable climate, we were in danger of starvation. Bukhara was rich in fruits such as apricots and grapes. However, by the time we arrived, the effects of the war were apparent and everything was scarce. Wartime normally results in famine but Russia compounded the problem by draining the cities it ruled of all their assets. Bukhara was no exception.

Disease was rampant and many of us suffered from a lack of

medical care. Russia was in the midst of fighting a war, with Stalin as its commander-in-chief. An example of his unfeeling determination to win was at the battle at Stalingrad, where his own soldiers were being slaughtered. When asked if they should retreat he stubbornly insisted: "Not one step back."Thousands of soldiers were killed in that bloodbath and many other required complicated and expensive medical attention. All available medical care and food were sent to soldiers fighting the war and consequently, drugs, doctors and food were extremely difficult to obtain.

While in Bukhara, we were free to scrape by to survive, meaning, we were not political prisoners forced into harsh labor as in Russia. I was young, nineteen or twenty, and wanted to find a productive job to occupy my time. I found a job in a Russian kindergarten teaching refugee children. The benefit of the job was not the salary, for that was meager, but the food. At lunch time the children received a piece of brown bread and we teachers got some too. We also had another luxury there that we had not had in Russia — candles to light up our "home" at night.

During our "spare" time we, the city dwellers, searched for food to sustain us. Every day we went to the marketplace to stand on lines for food. Each person was entitled to his food ration for the day. However the supply did not always last until the end of the line, for all we got was the army surplus. Often, after several hours of waiting for one loaf of bread, we would find there was none left by the time it was our turn. Furthermore, each line served only one product and so, after waiting several hours for a potato, we had to go wait just as long for some bread. Legally, we were supposed to pay for our wares in Russian rubles. However this money bought very little, for rubles were practically worthless and one would need a valise full of these bills just to buy some food. People began to find alternate solutions to the terrible inflation. The black market operated in earnest bartering clothes, quality foods and, most importantly, American dollars. These dollars were traded quietly because they were illegal tender. Another avenue we discovered was the use of gold coins. These small pieces were about the size of a dime but worth much more. Many refugees from large Russian cities brought suitcases of these coins along with them to exile.

Obtaining food, or the money to buy it, became the focus of our lives. I remember how my father would carefully divide one loaf of bread between all the members of my family. Each portion was precious so he tried to make them as even as possible. We hungrily devoured every last crumb awarded to us, even though this bread tasted like rocks.

My brother-in-law came up with a way to make money to buy more food. He decided to bake fresh white bread and sell it illegally. First we had to find a way to get plain flour, a commodity not freely sold. We approached a head of the government flour factory, for there were no private businesses. He was just a salaried government worker who also needed money to supplement his small income. He agreed to steal sacks of flour for us in return for a share of the profits. Everything was done with the utmost secrecy. My brother hollowed out a wall in the cellar and built an oven there. Each day he went downstairs and baked bread to sell. We were able to sell our homemade white bread for more money than the government-rationed bread because the quality was so much better. The government bread was tasteless and hard, while ours was soft and fresh. Speculators who had made money through illegal transactions with dollars were the ones who bought bread from us.

I became the messenger girl. Every day it was my job to go out to sell the bread. I would take a satchel filled with bread and stand on the corner to sell our goods. My heart pounded every minute that I stood there for fear that our business would be discovered. *Baruch Hashem, Hashem* watched over me and I was never caught. My family and I never ate the bread we baked. We could not afford to eat our profits, especially with the risk involved. With the money we earned by selling the bread, we were able to buy the government bread and some extra food beyond our meager rations. This too was illegal but out of necessity we risked it. Food could always be obtained on the black market if one could pay the price.

Besides bread, we were able to get rice and sometimes sugar. The sugar we bought came loose, without any containers. Since we had no bags, we used to fill up a hat or our pockets. Each grain of sugar was precious and we had to walk carefully to be sure not to spill even one grain. We also ate, strictly out of hunger, a food called *makuch*. It was a type of vegetable from which oil was squeezed and used for fuel. We ate the remaining husk, something that looked, smelled and tasted like coal.

We suffered so much from hunger and starvation that we spent whole days talking and thinking about food. Women, men and children had swollen stomachs from malnutrition. After eating the little we did have, we licked our fingers and touched them to the table, picking up any stray crumb we might have missed.

My niece was a small child of six at the time. Once, we were cooking soup out of a few carrots we bought on the black market. The poor child was so hungry that when no one was watching she took some of the carrots. I remember how upset we were because food was so scarce and the few carrots she took should have been stretched to serve several people.

❦ ❦ ❦

Shabbos in Bukhara was less of a trial than it had been in the labor camp. There we were forced to work on Shabbos while here we could take off and stay home for that day. I had two friends with me in Bukhara. One was the daughter of the Tshebiner *Rav*, and the other was Gitty Piller. Gitty and I had been classmates in seminary and there we rekindled our friendship. I had left all my notebooks from school in Poland but she had taken them along with her. It was a pleasure to be able to spend those Shabbos afternoons reviewing those uplifting lessons we had learned so long before.

We had to save money to buy extra bread in advance for Shabbos. Just having that extra food on the table was a special treat.

The living conditions were awful. Streets and houses were always dirty, as were the residents. Epidemics, plagues, and sicknesses were everyday affairs. People were dying in the streets of typhus, dysentery and other contagious diseases. I became sick with typhus and was hospitalized. My illness was characterized by an extremely high fever that sapped my appetite. Because I had no desire to eat, I put my bread ration under my pillow to save for when I would feel well enough to enjoy it. I never got to enjoy my hidden cache of food for while I slept the nurses stole my bread supply to satisfy their own hunger.

It was miraculous that we survived there for several years. Many people, my parents included, succumbed to the harsh living conditions and passed away. When my brother-in-law saw how many people were dying, he began to make a special list. On it he recorded the names of all the people who had died and on which day they were *niftar* (passed away). I asked him why he bothered to do this, since their graves were marked. He answered that just in case he met women who were not sure if their husbands were alive, he could allay their doubts with proof. Therefore, they would not be *agunos* and could remarry. Also, relatives might want to say *Kaddish* but would be unable to because of lack of proof of their relative's demise. My brother-in-law updated this list religiously. Unfortunately by the time we left it was very long.

These six years — from 1939, when we left Sanz, to 1945, when the war ended — were in truth lost years. We had so little learning or Torah study with us. However, there was so much *mesiras nefesh* (self-sacrifice) to just stay Jewish while keeping alive, we gained a lifetime of experiences to learn from.

♋   ♋   ♋

When the war ended, relief slowly began to seep into our lives. Even as early as the end of 1944 we began to receive packages from the United States. The Vaad Hatzalah under the leadership of Rabbi Eliezer Silver and Rabbi Elimelech Tress sent boxes of food and clothing. These packages contained storable food such as powdered milk and canned mackerel. There was some doubt among us as to whether this fish was kosher or not. Although some felt fish had to be kosher and we were in the greatest need of protein, we did not eat them. Instead we sold them to the non-Jews and used the money. They also sent old clothes. To us these were valuable for we were able to sell them for food and money on the black market. These packages were life lines that we eagerly awaited and rejoiced in when received. By then, if a Jew needed money he could get it. We began to see a light trying to shine through the darkness of our lives.

Among the first of our group to be able to leave Bukhara was the Tshebiner *Rav* and his family. The British ruling Palestine at the time did not want Jews to immigrate there and certification was hard to obtain. *Hashem* helped and the Tshebiner *Rav* procured certificates for my brother-in-law, sister, their children and my parents to emigrate to *Eretz Yisrael*. However, by the time they let us leave, my parents had died. Since my brother and I were only written on my parents' certificates, the government refused to let us use them to emigrate.

 With us in Bukhara was a group of about thirty *bachurim* from *yeshivos* such as Kletzk, Radin, and Mir. Throughout our stay in the prison camp and then in Bukhara they kept together, learning day and night. They risked their lives to be able to learn together. The Russians considered them an organized group — organized against the beloved mother country. They tried to break them up any way they could, sometimes even arresting some of them. Regardless of all obstacles these *bachurim* continued to learn, at times practically starving from hunger. By the end of our stay, only ten of the original thirty were left. Now that the war was over, they began to look for *shidduchim* (marriage partners), wanting to rebuild their lives.

In 1945 I was introduced to one of these *bachurim*, R' Hirsch Feldman, and we soon decided to get married. One of the packages from America contained a simple white dress. This became my wedding gown. Before I wore it, I wanted it to be fresh and clean, so I washed it. This, however, was a mistake because the dress shrunk and I was afraid I might not be able to wear it. I had to rewash the dress and let it dry on me, hoping it would stretch back to my size. Luckily it worked and I was able to wear the dress.

My wedding was held in the courtyard between two large buildings. All the Jews in the neighborhood came. For the meal, we served the contents of a package we had just gotten from America. People who barely knew us came to partake of the "delicacies" we provided. It was understood that although we were all starving, a *simchah* would only be complete if everyone had a chance to satisfy their hunger.

Until late in the night, probably early into the next morning, we listened to speeches, sang and danced. The *bachurim*, all friends of my husband, were so happy for us they sat and sang non-stop. In a way, my wedding was symbolic of new beginnings; the rebuilding of lives were starting. We knew our stay in Bukhara would soon come to an end.

Traveling to America

t was 1945 and the war was officially over. Poland was still a satellite of Russia and therefore we were allowed to leave Russia proper and go there. Lodz, always a center of Polish Jewry, was the city we decided to go to. My husband, brother and I set out with many other Jews to Poland. For a few years my husband had been working as a teacher and his meager salary paid for our train tickets.

During the ride, we told over all we had gone through, relieved that it was all behind us. We were eager to return to the friends and relatives we left, to tell them what had happened to us, to catch up on the seven years we lost. We were in for a great disappointment.

Poland, a country that had boasted of flourishing Jewish communities, was now desolate. Its pleasant scenery was replaced by rampant destruction. The relatives we left behind no longer existed. Big bustling Lodz was not the thriving Jewish community of years before; it was a haven for refugees.

We met many people from Radin, Slutsk, Kletzk and other places, all trying to pull their lives together and start over. The *chassidishe* element was also present. During the war many of the chassidic dynasties had been virtually wiped out. We met many Gerer and Alexander *chassidim* also trying to rebuild.

While we were there we received relief funds from the American Jewish Joint Distribution Committee. They set up a camp-size kitchen where refugees ate. It was there that I had my first taste of meat after seven years. The unity exhibited there was beautiful to witness. The kitchen was a cooperative effort and we all pitched in to cook for the weaker undernourished people.

My husband helped organize a *yeshivah* among the many refugees in Lodz. The Torah study going on helped rebuild our lives in earnest. Some people tried returning to their old hometowns but they were disappointed because usually everything was gone. We did not have the heart to stay there for long and tried to leave as soon as possible.

Mrs. Recha Sternbuch, a Swiss woman who dedicated her life to *pidyon shevuyim*, came to Poland and began working on obtaining immigration papers for us. Yeshiva Torah Vodaas of America was a government-recognized institution. They were allowed to give out papers recognizing *bachurim* as foreign students coming to study. Mrs. Sternbuch helped the *yeshivah* boys get papers, money and passports.

❦ ❦ ❦

After several weeks, many people began to leave Lodz for more pleasant, final destinations. We were unable to go straight to *Eretz Yisrael* or America and we detoured to Prague, Czechoslovakia. There we lived in the remains of former camps. We slept in large barrack-like buildings that had been used for inmates. The *yeshivah* set up a large kitchen where all the *bachurim* and families ate.

While in Prague my husband continued to firmly organize and establish his *yeshivah*. Classes included boys of all ages from all types of homes, backgrounds and situations. Some were orphans, while others had parents too upset or confused to know what to do with them. Some knew a lot while others knew very little. Our *yeshivah* had to cater to all these special, diverse personalities.

We were in Prague for only a few months when Mrs. Sternbuch again came to our aid. She provided us with passports and papers to go to France.

As in Lodz and in Czechoslovakia, my husband reestablished his *yeshivah*, serving as its head. The Jewish community that we met in Paris was very helpful. We received accommodations for the entire *yeshivah* from the Joint. The large beautiful building was surrounded by scenic fields and gardens. We were lucky to finally have so many spacious rooms and open lands. This palace was in the outskirts of Paris, not far away from Versailles. Since so many people — the families and *bachurim* of the *yeshivah* — were in this one building, each of the large rooms was divided into sections, with one section per family. We had one cook who took care of the task of feeding everybody.

We lived approximately one hour away from Paris, a considerable distance in those times. Consequently, we did not spend much time in the city.

We kept mostly to ourselves, becoming a close-knit group. For the time being, our situation was pretty good. I had little babies at the time and I enjoyed the fact that life was almost normal again. Nevertheless, we all knew that our stay in Paris was temporary and conversation usually centered around plans for the future.

❦ ❦ ❦

Shortly after our arrival, Israel gained its independence. Many refugees decided they wanted to rebuild their lives in *Eretz Yisrael*. Others obtained passports to America and proceeded to go there. We did not have the papers to emigrate from France and, for the time being, we stayed put. My husband was very occupied with the *yeshivah*, giving several *shiurim* and attracting *talmidim* (students) from all over. Conditions were favorable and we were in no great rush to leave.

However many of the older *bachurim* were more interested in settling down somewhere permanently and were impatient to move on. In August of 1950 we received our exit visas to emigrate from France. I wanted to move to *Eretz Yisrael*, but the state had just been formed and was very unsettled. Settlements were not yet built up and we did not have the money to be pioneers. Besides my husband had been requested to move his growing *yeshivah* to America. We left France after a total of about four and a half years.

❧ ❧ ❧

The Jewish Federation, with help from the Joint, provided us with a large boat. The Valendon was a Dutch ocean liner that had once been used for the army. After several days aboard this vessel, we arrived in New York. The HIAS, an organization to help refugees from Eastern Europe, provided us with hotel rooms on the East Side until we could find permanent accommodations.

After several weeks we moved to Flatbush, where the Mir Yeshiva reestablished itself. My husband's *yeshivah* dispersed among other *yeshivos* in New York, while he became *mashgiach* in Mir. The Jewish community we encountered consisted mostly of Sephardic Jews. The *Sephardishe* community was not what it is today. They did not provide their children with a *yeshivah* education, nor did they keep *kashrus* (kosher).

There were only a few religious schools. For girls, there was Bais Yaakov of Boro Park, elementary and high schools. There were several good *yeshivos* for boys such as Mir, Yeshivas Yitzchak Elchanany, Chaim Berlin and Torah Vodaas.

New York eventually became the center of *Yiddishkeit* in America. However, for us immigrants, there were many things to become accustomed to in this new land. America was so different from Europe. The language was unfamiliar to us and we had trouble communicating. Financially it was a very difficult situation. We often had to struggle to make an adequate living. We had to start over again on all fronts, without any parents or grandparents to look toward for guidance.

Rebbetzin Faiga Zaks

"My father was a very caring person,
and a concerned father.
Every winter night he came upstairs
to check that the rooms were warm enough,
so that we wouldn't catch colds.
He continued his nightly checks
until he was ninety years old
and the steps were too difficult for him."

Youngest child of Rabbi Yisroel Meir HaCohen, the Chafetz Chaim, and his wife Freida Miriam, Rebbetzin Faiga Zaks was born in Radin. During World War I, the family fled before the oncoming German army, returning in 1917. Shortly thereafter, she was wed to Rabbi Mendel Zaks. During World War II they fled to America. Rabbi Zaks held a prominent position on the staff of Yeshiva University until they moved to Israel in 1968. After her husband's death in 1974, R' Faiga Zaks continues to live in Israel.

Me and My Father

was born and raised in Radin, a small city in Poland. Being the youngest, I received a lot of attention from my family, especially my father. I remember how he used to sit with me at mealtimes coaxing me to eat. I was a picky eater and meal times were often a battle of wills.

I was a mischievous child, as children tend to be. Sometimes when my father was walking me home, I would run ahead impishly, trying to see if he would catch me. At a young age, I realized he was a *kohen* and would not enter a cemetery. I would run ahead and disappear into the cemetery, knowing full well that he could not follow me in. After a while I tired of my game and ran home.

One winter night, when I was only about five or six years old, I happened to get home later than usual. It was snowing hard and I rushed into the house to take off my coat. Once inside, I saw my father at the table learning.

"Did you make sure to close the front door well?" my father asked.

"I probably closed it well," I answered distractedly.

"Probably you did *not* close it well," answered my father. "Go outside and make sure it's closed."

I was tired and and cold and did not want to go out again.

"Tatty, I'm *sure* I closed the door," I protested.

"I'm sure you did not," he answered sternly.

I went to the door and saw he was right. I *had* forgotten to close the door, and by now the hall was slowly filling with snow. At first I couldn't even close the door. After a few minutes of pushing out the snow, the door closed and I went back inside.

"Do you see, *mamele*, how careful you must be with everything you do?" My father said when I came in. "Tomorrow the girl who helps clean the house would have had to clean up a big mess. Not only would you have caused extra *tzaar* (grief) to a working girl, but to a girl who is an orphan. Do you realize how many *aveiros* (sins) there are when you bring *tzaar* to an orphan, even when you are in the right? How much more so when you are wrong! You must be careful with even the smallest of your actions. If you have a doubt as to whether or not you did something right, it means you did not do it with the amount of thought you should have. Everything you do must be right, not maybe right or probably right." This was an important part of my upbringing. I was taught that every action one does must be carefully thought out, no "probably's". Before doing anything you must try to understand the outcome and base your actions on that.

Everything my father did was carefully considered. When I was about four years old, my mother brought me my first doll. My father took the doll from my hands and went into the kitchen. With a sharp knife, he carved out her eyes and the tip of her nose. I looked in tearful disbelief at my mutilated doll. Softly my father explained that a doll is like an idol; it must be made imperfect in order for it not to be considered an idol. When you know you are doing something right, you cannot take a child's tears into consideration. The children will learn that certain things are wrong and must not be tolerated regardless of how they might feel.

Along with his care in his every action was the importance my father attached to every word he said. I remember learning this lesson at a young age. Before my father would sell any of his *sefarim* (books), he made sure they were individually checked to ensure none of the pages were torn, stuck or misprinted. He wanted to make sure he did not take money for an imperfect *sefer*. I was on my way to visit a friend when my father stopped me at the door. "I have three sets of *Mishnah Brurah* that need to be checked over," he said. "I'll do it later," I answered as I put on my coat to go out.

"I need it now," he said firmly.

"When I come home, I'll check thirteen sets. Just let me go now, please?" I begged.

My father said nothing and I took that as permission to leave. I ran out before he could change his mind, mentally promising to check the *sefarim* when I would return.

Several hours later, I came home to find thirteen sets of *Mishnah Brurah* sitting on the table waiting to be checked.

"But, Tatty," I cried, "you gave me only three sets to check before. Why are there thirteen on the table now?"

"Yes," nodded my father, "I asked you to check only three sets but you said you would do thirteen when you returned. These are the thirteen sets you said you would do."

"But I didn't mean it literally. Everybody says things they don't really mean," I protested.

"Man is responsible for every word that comes out of his mouth. Being careful with what you say includes only saying what you mean. You said you would check thirteen sets of *Mishnah Brurah* when you came home and here they are," my father answered. That was one lesson I never forgot.

My father engaged a tutor for me when I was very young. He taught me to read and understand Hebrew in order to *daven* properly. This was the extent of my formal education. Nevertheless, I was an inquisitive child, always eager to learn more.

Every summer my oldest sister Sarah went to the country with her two daughters. I was only about seven years old, but I felt I was old enough to go with them to the country. I looked up to my two nieces who were older and more educated than I was. After a few days of persistent begging my father agreed to let me go. The weeks in the country flew by and soon I was home again.

A day or so after my arrival my father asked me to take a package of *sefarim* to the printer. The printer was the only man in Radin who knew how to write Russian. These *sefarim* were to be sent to Russia and my father wanted him to address the package.

"Tatty," I said, "I know how to write Russian."

"What!" My father was shocked. "Where did you learn to write Russian?"

"Well, when I went with Sarah to the country she hired a tutor for the girls. When they had their lessons, I sat in the corner and listened. It wasn't very hard and I caught on quickly," I replied. My father listened thoughtfully but said nothing.

A year passed and summer rolled around. I wanted to accompany my sister to the country as I had the previous year. Again, I begged my father for permission to go. This time my father was adamant, "A place where a Jewish girl learns to write Russian is not the place for you." That was the end of my country vacations.

Although I had very little formal education, I was always eager to learn. I tried to get my hands on any available literature and, through those books, taught myself several languages. I learned to read and write Polish, Russian, English, Hebrew and, naturally, Yiddish.

World War I

I was about eight years old when World War I broke out. It was shortly after Succos and the bitter Russian winter was already beginning to set in. Friday afternoon, my father decided it was not safe to stay in Radin, and we must go deeper into Russia, further away from a possible attack. As we were on the train, dusk began to set in. According to *halachah* we could have stayed on the train because it was for *pikuach nefesh* (saving a life) that we were traveling. However my father felt that since he and R' Elchonon Wasserman, who was accompanying us, looked so obviously like Jewish rabbis, their presence on a train on a Friday night would be a *chilul Hashem* (desecration of G-d's name). Therefore, ten minutes before sunset we all got off the train. That night we slept on the freezing cold ground outside the train station. My father took off his coat and covered me with it, trying to keep me warm. It was bitter cold and my father was afraid one of us might freeze in our sleep. He stayed up all night watching us, without a coat or jacket for warmth.

After Shabbos we took the train and settled in the town of Minsk. During the war years we settled in different towns, moving deeper and deeper into Russia. We lived in four or five different places, temporarily settling in each. In every town we rented a small furnished house for an indefinite period of time. We were finally able to go back to Radin in 1917.

Changes

One peaceful afternoon, as I was playing with my other twelve-year-old friends, my brother-in-law R' Hirsh Levenson came to visit. I pricked my ears as I overheard what they were talking about.

"I have the perfect *shidduch* (match) for Faigele," said R' Hirsh to my father.

When my mother heard this she fainted. A *shidduch* for her twelve-year-old "baby?!" Nonplused my father reassured her he would not force me to marry anyone. However, from that day on, I was observed in a new light for it wouldn't be long before they would have to look seriously for a suitable match.

My father did not actually consider *shidduchim* until I was sixteen years old. That year is clear in my mind for many reasons. My sister's beloved husband, R' Hirsh Levinson, passed away a few months before making a deep impression on all of us. Around that time my mother took sick and it was my responsibility to run the house. I was young and strong and certain that I would stay that way. Typhus was a killer disease at the time and many of our friends and neighbors succumbed to it. As I went from house to house helping those who were sick, I didn't really think that I could also catch the disease. For several weeks, I helped cook and clean not only at my house, but at the houses of sick friends and neighbors as well. One morning, I woke up hot, feverish, unable to even get out of bed. The typhus fever made me delirious as I tossed and turned in bed. Doctors despaired of my recovery; the only one to turn to was *Hashem*. My father added on the name "Chaya," hoping the changed name would be of help. Suddenly, the fever broke and my very slow recovery began. When I became strong enough my father told me how sick I had been, and that my returned health was literally a miracle.

I was seventeen when my engagement to R' Mendel Zaks was announced. At the time we had not yet returned to Radin but we were settled back home in time for the *chassunah*. We were married outside the *Bais Medrash* and then went home for the meal. There were ten men at the meal, the family and one or two guests. The neighbors all came in to wish *mazel tov* and be present at the *sheva brachos* (blessings recited at the end of the wedding feast).

My father promised us three years of support at his table. To make sure everything was perfectly understood, my father clearly wrote out exactly for what he was taking responsibility. The contract stated that he would provide us with three years of room and board. This included our food necessities (not extras) and a place to sleep for present and future members of the family. If, for any reason, he could not fulfill the agreement, he was not required to sell his pillows, blankets or tables to support us. The pillows, blankets and table were the extent of his valuable worldly possessions. Although we would never have thought of asking my parents to sell all they owned to support us, my father wanted to make sure everything was clearly, "*halachically*," agreed upon.

We moved into the upstairs of my parent's house. Our new home consisted of one large room divided in half. One side was for me and my husband and the other side was for children *im yirtzeh Hashem* (G-d willing). Before giving us our rooms, my father approached me with a choice.

"It would be smarter for you to take the downstairs rooms," he said. "I am an old man, and I don't have any reason to go up and down the stairs often. You, on the other hand, will *im yirtzeh Hashem* have children. Day and night you will have to run up and down the stairs to prepare bottles and care for the children. It will be much easier for you downstairs."

I was amazed at his remarkable unselfishness. Firmly, I answered, "Tatty, I am young and strong. It is easy for me to go up and down stairs many times. You are getting older and it is getting harder for you to walk. It is more important for you to have the ground-floor rooms than me."

My father was a very caring person, and a concerned father. Every winter night he came upstairs to check that the rooms were warm enough so that we wouldn't catch colds. He continued his nightly checks until he was ninety years old and the steps were too difficult for him.

Moving On

n 1933 my father passed away. We continued to live in Radin where my husband was one of the *roshei yeshivah*. He saw that the situation in Europe was precarious at best. On one of his fund-raising missions to America he applied for "First Papers" for the family. These were alien applications towards residency in the United States in case we would be forced to leave Europe. He urged my brothers to do the same for their families but they refused to believe such drastic preparations were necessary.

While my husband was away, the Russians invaded Radin. It was *Simchas Torah* of 1937 when they arrived in the city. They wanted a peaceful takeover where the citizens would welcome their occupation. They brought chocolate and candies, distributing them to the children they passed. But they fooled no one; we knew their arrival meant trouble and we must leave.

Rebbetzin Faiga Zaks with her mother and her two oldest sons

Right after *Yom Tov* I began packing our belongings. Amidst the frenzied preparations I heard a knock at the door. Standing outside were several Russian officials. My heart thumped loudly as I admitted them into the house.

With smiles on their faces and honey in their words they stated their offer. If we accept Russian citizenship they would let us keep our house, possessions and life style. If not ... My husband had always been a fiery anti-Communist even before the concept was popular. He felt that it was better to actually fight the Russians than accept them. His words echoed in my mind as I stared at the Russian officers, their cruel calculating eyes belying the smiles on their lips.

I looked straight at them and said, "I want to raise my children as Jews. Your government won't tolerate religion especially our religion. I won't tolerate your government." Obviously angered at my response, they left quickly.

That night we finished packing and fled to Vilna. Shortly thereafter, the Yeshiva in Radin was disbanded by the Russians and many of the *bachurim* sent to Siberia. We cried and mourned over those who were sent away. Little did we realize that although they endured several years of hard labor, they survived. The other Jews of Radin perished when the Germans occupied the city.

We stayed in Vilna for two years. My husband was sitting and learning and we managed to scrimp by with what we had.

In 1939, the war broke out and the multitudes of Jews in Vilna began looking for ways to leave. *Baruch Hashem* my husband was far sighted enough to get us First Papers. These enabled us to get transit visas to the United States through Japan.

We boarded a train on the Trans-Siberian Railroad en route to Vladivostok. I knew that it would be difficult to get kosher food and therefore, instead of keeping money or jewels, I sold everything and bought as much food as possible. We carried aboard with us an entire pail of jam, cans and cans of sardines, rolls and rolls of salami. I even brought along a "canning stove." This was a small portable type of stove used to warm up small meals. Everyday one person per family was allowed to leave the train to buy bread. However, were it not for the food we brought along, we and many others would have suffered much more.

To travel in Europe, especially during wartime, you needed many different types of papers. There were personal identification papers, working papers, passports, visas and various other official forms one dared not travel without. Many people could not get the necessary papers and therefore had forgeries made. Some of these were such bad forgeries any civilian could have spotted them. At least once a day, the Russian officers boarded the train to inspect our papers. Each day that we passed inspection was clearly a miracle.

In Vladivostok we boarded a cattle boat to take us across the Straits of Japan to Kobe, Japan. I remember spending Purim on that boat. We all gathered together to listen as my husband read the *megillah*. Among those with us were the Amshinover Rebbe, Reb Dovid Lipshitz and Reb Yisroel Chaim Kaplan. Although we were physically weak and bereft, Torah learning was constant.

We arrived in Japan shortly after Purim. The route of our travels took us over the International Dateline, causing several problems. We, a group of about seventy families, had no contact with the free world. The question arose as to what the proper date was and we had no way of communicating to anyone who could give us a definite answer. Among the *rebbeim* with us, most felt certain that the dates we were counting were accurate. However, there were those who felt that we might be one day off and therefore were keeping Shabbos on the wrong day. They decided to keep two days of Shabbos just to be sure.

My husband had us keep only one day but on the second day we avoided any unnecessary work. The Amshinover Rebbe was one of

Rebbetzin Faiga Zaks

those people who kept two days of Shabbos. I would cook for him and others and send my children to deliver food to them.

Giving them food on their second day of Shabbos was not a problem for my family. The problem arose on the day we kept Shabbos. The Yokania Hotel, the new large luxurious hotel where we stayed, was owned by *goyim*. In the rooms we rented there was no question about carrying — it was perfectly permissible. However, we had no *eruv* to enable us to carry from one room to another. We had no choice but to let the little children deliver the food on Shabbos; it was a question of *pikuach nefesh*.

According to the hotel regulations I was not allowed to use my canning stove in the room. I used to hide it under the bed until the *cholent* was cooked. Then I covered the pot several times with towels and hid it from the maid. Once, she walked in unannounced. I covered the pot like a baby and put it next to my daughter who was already in bed. She never gave the bundle a second glance.

Luckily, we did not have to stay in Japan long. Just after Pesach we received certification to emigrate to America. We traveled by boat across the Pacific to Seattle, Washington. A family by the name of Gershon took us in for the few days we stayed there. From there we took a train to New York State. We lived in an apartment on West Side Manhattan, just below Reb Aharon Kotler and his family.

Starting life anew in America was very hard. We were in a foreign land, knew nothing of the language or way of life. My husband had difficulty finding a job. He was offered a position as a *rosh yeshivah* in Montreal. Yet New York was destined to be a Torah center and he did not want us to move to Montreal. And so, for several years, he stayed in Montreal, coming home just for *yomim tovim*.

We soon saw that this was not a good arrangement. My husband returned home, his job prospects still dim. He then received an offer to join the staff of Yeshiva University. Now we faced a dilemma: To stay in New York without a job would mean living off *tzedakah* (charity); yet, how could he teach in a *yeshivah* whose ideas he did not support? And yet, there were many *talmidei chachamim* on the staff of Yeshiva University. He decided that this decision was too complex for him to make on his own.

My husband met with the most renowned *rabbanim* in America at that time — Rav Henkin, Rav Yaakov Kaminetzky, Rav Moshe Feinstein, Rav Aharon Kotler and others — and presented his problem. They felt that he could and should accept the position.

The position they wanted him for was one of a *bochen*. He was to constantly test and examine the students and the *rebbeim* to make sure they were on the level they should be. He would walk into a class, sit down and follow the *shiur* in *Gemara* without having the *sefer* before him and without preparation. Pen and paper in hand, he graded the *rebbe* and the *talmidim*, sometimes even adding his own corrections and comments after class.

Although Yeshiva University was very happy with the work my husband was doing, he was never entirely satisfied with the school itself. Their differences in views created a gap that was hard to bridge. For many years he tried to leave. Finally, in 1968 we moved to *Eretz Yisrael* where my husband was able to sit and learn until his death in 1974.

Rebbetzin Zlata Ginsburg

> "All in all, this is a typical picture of life in a Polish shtetl over half a century ago. The residents were simple Yidden, great Yidden, living together and, most importantly, learning together, using their lives to serve Hashem."

Rebbetzin Zlata Malka Ginsburg was born in the Lithuanian town of Kelm. Her father, Reb Chatzkel Levenstein later joined Rav Aharon Kotler's *yeshivah* in Kletzk as *mashgiach*. A few years later, she and her family moved to the *yeshivah* in Mir, Poland, where she married Rabbi Ephraim Mordechai Ginsburg.

When Mir came under Russian hegemony at the beginning of World War II, Rabbi and Rebbetzin Ginsburg joined her parents and many of the *yeshivah bachurim* and *rebbeim* in fleeing, first to Vilna and ultimately to Shanghai. With the end of the war the *yeshivah,* the Ginsburg family among them, began to rebuild in New York.

Shtetl Life

I was born in Kelm, a *shtetl* in Lithuania. There my father learned in the *yeshivah*, the Talmud Torah of Kelm.

My father, mother, sister, and I lived in a small house, together with my grandmother. Families in Europe were very close and we lived in close proximity of aunts, uncles and cousins.

Neither of my parents had ever been completely healthy. My father was frail looking and sickly even as a young man, at times coughing up blood. My mother was often bedridden and I would take over the housework.

I know that nowadays doctors say that many eggs are unhealthy because of their cholesterol content. However, my father always felt they were a healthy food, rich in energy. He ate at least two eggs a day and when he became sick with lung problems, eight eggs a day. My father, who had been sick since he was young, lived *Baruch Hashem* until close to ninety.

Because it was cheap and "filling," bread was a major part of our diet. Our bread was hard and not easily digestible. We waited a whole week for the delicious challah made of the best flour and eggs. Because my father was sickly he could not digest the hard bread we usually had. My mother used to save challah from Shabbos to serve my father during the week.

Although we ourselves were poor, we often had guests even less fortunate than us. One night, as we sat down to eat, our guest demanded that he be served challah. Without pausing to consider, my father gave him his portion and took some plain bread for himself. Later my mother reproached him. saying, "Why did you give away the challah I had saved for you? Our guest was not a sick man. He is a poor man who should have been happy to eat what the rest of us ate." My father answered simply but firmly, "If a poor man wants roast duck, and there is any way to provide it, you must provide it." That ended any argument.

Nowadays, our streets are lined with cars, and the "horse and buggy" era seems to have been at least a century ago. In Poland, less than fifty years ago, automobiles were a luxury only for the very rich. In my *shtetl* there was one car, a taxi in which you could travel to meet the train. Other than that, in the summer there were horse drawn carriages and in the winter, horse drawn sleds.

One modern convenience I remember not having was electricity. I still recall that when I was about five years old, our only source of light was a lantern. In Mir, although we did have electricity, the power was quite weak. The bulbs were small — maybe fifteen watts — but they provided us with most of our light. The electricity was used for nothing else because any other appliance, which no one owned anyway, could not run on such weak power.

When I was a child, pencils were non-existent; I was taught how to dip the "pen" into home-made ink and write with it. As I got older, inventions such as pencils developed. Even though they were never considered valuable in America, in Poland they were precious. Once, I was in the *yeshivah* and I saw a *bachur* crawling on the floor on his hands and knees. He had dropped his pencil, and although it was unseemly for a serious student to crawl on the floor for anything, it was not considered strange to "stoop" to search for so valuable a commodity.

The life of a *yeshivahman* in Poland was usually one of such poverty that it is barely comprehensible to one growing up in America. Our wardrobes consisted of about two outfits for the weekdays and one for Shabbos. We were lucky enough to obtain boxes of dresses from American cousins, and those clothes received were taken to the seamstress to be remade into outfits for us. Sometimes there would be something special like a pair of boots or a coat. The winters in Poland were bitterly cold and warm coats were priceless. Once, one of the boxes yielded a fine quality, very warm sealskin coat. For many years I used the warm coat until, one day, my father announced that he had saved up enough money to buy a new coat. I had never had a new coat of my own, and, being the oldest, I really was entitled to it. However, Yocheved was younger and it was more important to her than to me. Therefore I forfeited my priority as eldest and agreed to let Yocheved have the new coat. I survived, none the worse, with my old coat, until we had enough money for a new one.

❦ ❦ ❦

When I was a young girl of twelve, my father wanted to reinforce the importance of helping my mother in the house. He made an agreement with me; if I would wash the kitchen floor

The Levenstein Family

every Friday afternoon, after a while he would buy me a present. For several months I diligently made sure to complete my job. One night he announced that because I had been helping in the house so conscientiously, the next day he would purchase a watch for me as a prize.

To fully comprehend my excitement you must understand the rarity of gifts. The concept of "birthday presents" was a secular idea, foreign to us. On Chanukah we received only practical gifts, nothing frivolous as a watch. This was a real treat that I felt I had earned.

The next morning I jumped out of bed, a high spirited skip in my step. Cheerfully, I sat down to breakfast, my anticipation mounting. My mother prepared hot cocoa for breakfast. As she served me a cup, I accidently spilled it on my wrist. The shock of the boiling hot liquid coursing down my wrist made me scream out in agony. In pain and confusion I grabbed the nearest towel and started rubbing my wrist, trying to make the hurting stop. As I lifted the towel it peeled off the top layer of the burned skin. By now the house was in an uproar, everyone contributing their advice as to what I should do. A *bachur* from the *yeshivah* walked in just then.

"Pouring ink on a burn takes away the pain," he advised.

By now I was willing to try anything. Ink was duly poured on my wrist as we waited for results. Now, it's possible that when one received a first degree burn, and the outer skin is only slightly burned, ink can relieve the pain. However, my burn was more complicated because I had accidentally rubbed out that upper layer of skin. As ink seeped into my wrist, it began to swell up. Within an hour, it was practically double its usual size. When my father saw this, he immediately took me to see a doctor.

The doctor pensively examined my wrist, not saying a word. Finally, he spoke, "I have some medicine for you to apply to the skin. If the medicine helps and the swelling goes down, your wrist will be okay and you will be a very lucky girl. If the swelling does not decrease, you must go to see a specialist in Warsaw. He might be able to save the hand but if not, it must be amputated."

As we left the office, I was silent and scared, hoping that the worst would not happen. *Baruch Hashem* my wrist began to heal and within a few days all I was left with was a scar.

Now that my wrist was better, I expected to receive my watch. "No," my father said, "the fact that you burned your left wrist, where you wear a watch, on the day you were supposed to receive the watch, is a sign that it is not for you. You should realize that helping your mother in the house is something you should do without being promised a prize!"

That was the end of my watch. I did not receive a watch until after my marriage but that is another story. [Upon my marriage, I did not receive any presents other than the actual wedding ring. I used to tease my husband about buying me a watch.

"A watch!" he answered. "I would think that a daughter of Reb Chatzkel would not need something as frivolous as a watch."

"Reb Chatzkel's daughter is a human being too," I retorted.

This teasing went on for a while. One day, my husband decided that he wanted to go to Brisk to meet the *gaon* Reb Velvel, the Brisker Rav. In Brisk he went to visit Reb Yisroel Chaim Kaplan, the son-in-law of R' Yeruchem Levovitz. When he was in the house he happened to be talking to the rebbetzin.

"Rebbetzin," he asked, "I can't understand my wife. She was brought up in the house of the *Mashgiach*, without luxury, and yet she seems to really want a watch as a wedding present."

"What," she exclaimed, "do you mean to say you never bought her any type of wedding present?!! Every girl from every home wants . . . no she *needs*, a present from her *chassan*. Go out right now and buy her a watch."

He immediately went to a local store and bought the best watch he could afford. It cost thirty *zlotys*, a tremendous amount of money at the time, but once he realized how important it was to me, the money no longer mattered. — Ed.]

❦ ❦ ❦

Admittedly, it was not the easiest life, but nevertheless life in a Polish *shtetl* was very pleasant. It was like living in a *frum* bungalow colony all year long. Almost everyone we had contact with was Jewish, and we rarely ever saw a non-Jew in the street. Even when we ventured to a larger city on occasion, we rarely communicated with the Poles we saw there.

The shops, small businesses and groceries were owned and operated by *frum* Jews. The Polish peasants lived on the outskirts and came into town only on market day. The only non-Jews we came into daily contact with were the woodchoppers, water-carriers and maids.

If ever we saw a *goy* in town at night, or at a time when he shouldn't have been there, we cringed in fear. Even though we provided these peasants with their livelihoods and prosperity, they hated us. We could feel their anti-Semitism whenever we were in their midst. We recognized the malice behind their smiles.

One day a week in every *shtetl* was market day. In Kelm it was Thursday, in Mir it was Monday, but no matter what the day, market day was an event. Early in the morning the horse drawn wagons poured into town from the neighboring Polish villages. The Poles brought with them their livestock and wares for sale. One could buy chickens, eggs, animals (meat), ducks, turkey and butter. They also came to trade horses and oxen with the city's residents. With the money they earned from their produce the Poles went shopping in the Jewish stores in town. They bought material for clothes, ready-made shoes, and other foodstuffs. Some of the Poles who conducted business profitably spent the rest of the day in the Polish kiosk, enjoying themselves.

❦ ❦ ❦

As in any town, big or small, there were occasional breaks in the daily routine. One Friday afternoon, after I had taken my bath for Shabbos, an excited cry rang through the town. "Dancing bear!

Come watch the famous dancing bear!" We had no zoos, circuses or other amusements that you might find in a big city such as Warsaw. Occasionally a Pole would come to town bringing a trained bear, monkey or elephant. Everyone would crowd around to watch the animal perform its tricks. People would throw a coin in the man's hat in appreciation of the spectacle. "Dancing bear! Come watch the dancing bear." I ran outside hoping to get close enough for a good view. In my haste I did not watch where I was going. Suddenly I felt something pulling at my ponytail. I tried to turn around to see who was in back of me, but my head was somehow imprisoned. By now there was a crowd of people around me laughing and pointing at my head. I looked up and saw a giant bear towering over me, my ponytail in his mouth. The first thing I did was panic, screaming and crying, trying to pull my hair away. Unfortunately, everyone else, the bear included, thought it was very funny and was enjoying the sight. Realizing I was genuinely afraid, the bear trainer shouted some kind of command, and the bear let go. I ran home as fast as I could, blubbering incoherently to my mother.

That Shabbos I was the town celebrity. When we went out for our usual Shabbos walk, I felt everyone's eyes on me as they whispered to each other, "Look, that is the girl whose hair was eaten by the bear."

All in all this is a typical picture of life in a Polish *shtetl* over half a century ago. The residents were simple *Yidden*, great *Yidden*, living together and most importantly, learning together, using their lives to serve *Hashem*.

Kelm . . . Kletzk

In Kelm my father had no official position in the *yeshivah*. We lived from day to day, I am not quite sure how. When I was eight years old my father was offered a job of temporary Mashgiach in Mir Yeshiva. R' Yeruchem Levovitz was leaving for an indefinite period of time and they wanted my father to fill the gap.

Accepting this position posed several problems. At that time Poland and Lithuania were enemies and communication was illegal and regarded as treasonous. My father was from Warsaw and was therefore a Polish citizen with a legal passport. Several years before

Nechama Leiba, the wife of R' Hirsch Brody, R' Chatzkel's Rebbe is sitting with a visitor to Kelm.

he had had a Lithuanian passport made up for himself. It was illegal to have a passport from enemy countries because one could not be a citizen of both. However, by carefully using these two passports my father could go from Lithuania to Poland. While in Lithuania he showed his Lithuanian passport and while in Poland he showed his Polish passport. Yet all the time that the two documents were on his person he was in danger because if they were found the punishment could be death.

At the time, my sister and I were small children, and my mother was weak. We lived with my maternal grandmother who was quite old. We were all Lithuanian citizens and did not have double passports. It was too dangerous to try to move all of us to Poland for a position my father might not have for long anyway. Therefore, we stayed in Kelm while my father left to Mir.

Days stretched into weeks, weeks stretched into months, months stretched into years. Those years were very hard. Since communication was illegal it was impossible to send letters directly to each other. We had to send the letters to Germany, which was a neutral country at that time. We addressed the letters to a special agency, *Helfsfarein fun de Deitchishe Yidden*, in Berlin. From there they sent the letters to Poland or from Poland to Lithuania. This system worked well, however, because the letters had to go through so many channels, they took a long time to arrive at their destination. Everyday we waited anxiously for a letter. My mother cried silently, the worry etched in her face, waiting for those letters to come. I could not take her pain and sadness. Everyday I paced around nervously saying "*Ribbono Shel Olam*, help my father in Poland. Help my mother by sending those letters quickly. Please *Hakadosh Baruch Hu*, help us and the next time I have a penny I'll put it in the *pushke* (charity box)." The happiness and relief we felt upon receiving a letter cannot be imagined but it was soon replaced with anxiety for the next message.

For three long years, from when I was eight until I was eleven, I did not see my father. Finally the letter bearing the good news arrived. Reb Yeruchem was returning to Mir and my father was returning home to his family.

❦   ❦   ❦

At that time my father was offered positions as *mashgiach* in several *yeshivos*. Reb Aharon Kotler invited him to join him in Kletzk. This was a permanent offer and therefore my whole family would have to move to Poland. My mother's mother, who had lived with us for many years, was eighty-six. She did not have the strength or the health to make the journey to Kletzk. Although it meant giving up a good position and returning to Kelm where he had no livelihood, my father did not accept the job.

My father treated my grandmother like a son treats his natural mother. Every morning he woke up at six o'clock to wash her *negel vasser* and feed her some cake and milk. *Hakadosh Baruch Hu* blessed her with old age. She was eighty-nine when she died. After her death my father accepted the job in Kletzk.

The move to Kletzk involved a potentially dangerous journey. First my father went to Warsaw to make the necessary arrangements. He used his double passports and arrived there safely. My mother, sister and I went to Danzig, a neutral city in Germany. We were able to use our regular Lithuanian passports to get there but we still lacked the proper papers to enter Poland. For two months we lived in a small furnished apartment, waiting for further instructions. All that time my father was trying to get us the proper affidavits to legally cross the border. After a while he realized that this was unlikely and began to work on an alternate plan.

His brothers, whom he stayed with in Warsaw, helped devise a dangerous route by which we could steal across the border. My father wanted to go back to Danzig to get us himself but they convinced him that the journey would be too much of a strain on his health. One of my uncles offered to go in his place. It was February when he met us in Danzig. The plan was to steal across the border at night when we were least likely to get caught. We could not ride on a horse-drawn sled because we were going through heavily wooded forests where a horse and sled could not pass. Besides, it would make too much noise and might draw attention to us.

It was ten o'clock at night when we started out. Polish winters are notoriously cold, and Polish winter nights are absolutely unbearable. For hours we walked stealthily through the forests trying hard not to stumble or make a noise that would possibly draw a soldier to investigate. We could not afford strong leather boots; our boots were made of a woolen leg attached to a piece of wool — not protection enough for the cold. Along the way the bottom of my sister's boot slipped off, and since we could not stop to fix it, she continued to walk without anything covering her feet. Her foot became frostbitten from walking so long in the snow. Ever since, she has had trouble with her foot, a constant reminder of that journey.

From ten o'clock at night until six in the morning we walked, barely stopping to rest. Because we were unsure of the area, we had two guides accompanying us through the forest and over the border. Finally we reached a small town just over the border and into Poland. We were relieved to have made it safely thus far, but our journey was not over yet. We paid the guides for their job and they left us at an inn near the train station. For four hours we sat in the lobby waiting for the train to take us to Warsaw.

It was a few minutes to candle lighting when we walked into my relatives' home. My father clasped his hands together fervently exclaiming, "*Baruch Hashem!*" He rushed towards us, took hold of the hands of me and my sister, and danced us across the room. I can still remember that Shabbos, the *simchah* we felt being safely together at last.

Chinuch: More Than Just School

n Kelm, there was a single *frum* elementary school called Shulamis. It had been started by a young man learning in the Kelm Yeshiva. In the morning we were taught *limudei kodesh* (Jewish studies) by men and in the afternoon *limudei chol* (secular studies) by women. The curriculum resembled that of today's schools.

When I was in the fifth grade my father went to a parent-teachers' conference. My teacher of secular studies was very excited about my class performance and raved about my work, telling my father that I had potential to become a professor. That was my last day in school. Having no wish for his daughters to be professors or influenced by a teacher with those aspirations, my father took me and my sister out of the school immediately. For the next couple of years I had private tutors for *limudei kodesh* and Russian language.

It says, "חנוך לנער על פי דרכו, *Educate each child in his own way*," and now I see how my father practiced this. He let me use my intellectual capabilities by letting me help in the running of a nearby grocery. My sister was very talented with any type of sewing or needlework, so she worked as an apprentice to a seamstress where she learned the trade. We both benefited according to our capabilities.

I was fourteen when my father obtained the position in Kletzk. There were no Jewish high schools and the only alternative was public school. My father did not want to send me there but he felt it was important for a girl to have some form of higher education. Therefore, although it was expensive, he engaged a tutor to instruct me in science, mathematics and language. I was the only girl in the *shtetl* who did not go to public school for my father had strict views as to how to educate his daughters and he was willing to pay for them. The tutor came twice a week and during the remaining days of the week I had to complete the homework he assigned. My father personally taught me *limudei kodesh*.

My father always kept up with my schoolwork, praising me when I excelled and rebuking me when I achieved less than he expected. During the 1920's there was a world-wide depression. In Europe it was known as the crisis, a period in which poverty was rampant. In studying the situation I was assigned a paper to complete. I wrote an epic poem titled "The Crisis" which depicted this world-wide problem. My father was quick to praise my work, as he always was when it was warranted. He felt it was important to understand world affairs and politics, and my grasp of the situation pleased him.

Sometimes, my father gave his own "assignment." He handed me a notebook and a promise: If I wrote one *hashgacha-pratis* event that happened each day, after several weeks he'd buy me a prize. Sure enough, as I filled my little notebook I earned my rewards. Even though we were poor and money was tight, he was willing to spend the money to teach me how to appreciate *hashgachas Hashem* (G-d's special providence).

One lesson my father instilled in me as a child was to fear *gehinnom* (hell). He taught that in this world we are judged by *Hashem* with His *midas harachamim* (attribute of mercy) together with his *midas hadin* (strict justice). However, in the World to Come *Hashem* passes judgment without his *midas harachamim* and this judgment is fiery hot. To impress this upon me further my father used a parable. He said that two cats stand at the entrance of *gehenim*. At night, the cat's eyes are very bright, piercing and predatory. These two cats have eyes that look like a consuming fire and they seem ready to pounce upon any person within reach. Until this day I not only possess a distinct fear of *gehinnom* but I have an intense dislike of cats. In today's world we are soft with children and they hardly hear of *gehinnom* until they advance into school. I grew up with this fear implanted in me and it has stayed with me until today.

My father used to read to us the *Igeres Hagra* the famous letter of the Vilna Gaon that he wrote to his children. "העולם הזה דומה לשותה מים מלוחים, *This world is compared to drinking salty water.*" One can never quench his thirst with salty water but always wants more. People in this world are never happy because the more they have the more they want. As I look at the world today I see how true it is. In Europe we had so little but we were happy with much less. Here in America everyone has so much, and yet we are less happy than the *Yidden* then in Poland.

When I was little my father wanted to learn more with me. He would suggest a walk or a conversation but I gave into the ignorance of my youth and would make one excuse after another. Now I can only look back and regret the opportunities I lost.

Mir

 was seventeen years old when we moved to Mir. The entire town of Mir had, maybe, a thousand men. Geographically speaking, Mir was practically nonexistent, a mere speck on a map. However in *Hashem's* map of the world, Mir must have taken up a lot of space. It was a town dominated by the *yeshivah*, with its illustrious *roshei yeshivah* and many *talmidim*. The atmosphere was *heimishe* (homey) and everyone knew and cared for everyone else.

The city was not only Jewish but generally observant of the *Shabbos* as well. There was only one man in the *shtetl* who was known to be a *mechalel Shabbos* (desecrator of Shabbos) publicly. A carpenter by trade, he was a self-proclaimed Bundist, a type of Communist. None of us had much to do with him for he was more or less shunned by the *yeshivah* community. Any other desecrators of Shabbos were rebellious youths who would only dare to do so privately.

The city was filled with *bachurim*, *kollel* (seminary) students and *rebbeim* connected with the *yeshivah*. The others, too, led lives centered around Torah. The doctors, lawyers, grocers, shoemakers and proprietors of any businesses were *frum* Jews. Most of them would work only half the day, enough to support their families, and devote the remainder of the day to learning Torah. Frequently the women would take over their husbands' stores, often surrounded by the children too young for school. Young girls would be pulled out of school before graduation in order to help out at home or in the family business.

The *shtetl* of Mir was composed of exactly five streets, with no sidestreets or alleys. Each street was a wide dirt road with sidewalks and houses on either side. The market place was the center of town, the various streets protruding from it.

The *yeshivah* was situated in the middle of Wyaska Gass. Rav Kamai, *Rav* of Mir, lived on the same block. He acted as the *posek*

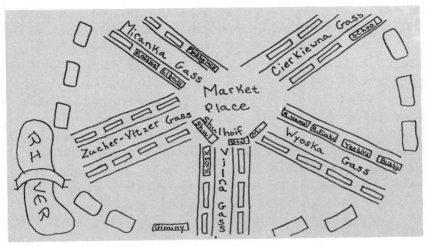

Map of the town of Mir

(halachic decider) of the city, and he said a *shiur* in the *yeshivah* several times a week. Next door to him lived Rav Leizer Yudel Finkel, *Rosh Yeshivas* Mir. It was he who led the *yeshivah* spiritually, with his uplifting *shiurim*, and physically, by seeing to the health and welfare of all the *bachurim*. My family and I lived further down the block, still in close proximity of the *yeshivah*.

The *mashgiach*, Reb Yeruchem Levovitz, lived on Miranka Gass, near the market place. He learned in Kelm, as my father did, and was *mashgiach* of Mirrer Yeshiva for over twenty years, turning the *yeshivah* into a center of *mussar* (the study of ethics). Towards the middle of the street was the post office. Actually, it wasn't very active, for it took two weeks for a letter to go from one small *shtetl* to another. Letters traveling overseas would be guaranteed *not to* reach their destination for at least two months. Therefore, people didn't write to each other very often and the mail business was very slow. Next door to the post office was the local library. There one could find books by the famous Polish and Jewish authors. It was run by the more secular minded Jews of Mir and some of the books reflected their modern views. For a small fee one could borrow several books to read over a short period of time.

There was one public school in the *shtetl* for all school age children. Polish law required everyone to attend school for at least the lower grades. There was a small Talmud Torah for the Jewish boys, but the girls had no choice but to attend this public school. The school was at the end of Cierkiewna Gass, near the homes of most of its pupils. The non-Jews lived on the outskirts of the city in little villages surrounded by forests.

On the border of the lower half of the market place was the *Shulhaif*. This was a clump of *shuls* and *batei medrash* situated near each other. The major *shul* was a large building where the more prestigious *baalei batim* spent time learning Torah. The other two buildings were called Bais Medrash Hagadol and Bais Medrash HaKaton.There learned the poorer members of the community who eked out their living by being craftsmen or small-scale shopkeepers. However, no matter what station in life, everyone set aside time to learn somewhere. Just as the cycle of the Jewish year is dominated by *yomim tovim*, daily life was dominated by Torah.

⚘ ⚘ ⚘

The *yeshivah* was the backbone of the small town of Mir. With a population of about two thousand people, five hundred were young men learning in the *yeshivah*. Students came from all over the world. There were about sixty *bachurim* from countries such as Belgium, England and Switzerland who came from far away to absorb the learning and *sevivah* (atmosphere) of Mir. Of all the *yeshivos* in Poland, Mir was best known for its international students.

In the late 1920's we had some very interesting newcomers to Mir. A young *kollel* student and his wife came from America to learn in the *yeshivah*. Reb Nachum Dovid Herman and his wife were the first Americans I had ever seen and were consequently objects of curiosity. They must have been pleased for shortly thereafter his sister and brother-in-law, Rav Chaim Scheinberg and his wife, joined them. I remember when they first came to my house. My sister and I hovered in the background trying to catch a glimpse of the "Americans." The young man talked to my father while his wife stood near his side. She wore a long black velvet coat with a genuine fox collar. We gaped in awe at what was the most impressive coat we had ever seen. Our impressions of America as a land of riches had begun to form.

Unlike *yeshivos* of today, Mir had no dormitories for the *bachurim* to lodge in, nor any kitchens or dining facilities. A system was established that would give these young men room and board while still helping them retain their independence. Upon arriving in Mir, the newcomer was assigned a house to board in run by a *balebuste* (landlady). Every boy received an allowance, a type of note, from the *yeshivah*, for food. It was redeemable for approximately two pounds of meat, with the fat and bones, and twelve pounds of bread. They were also given a *chalukah*, a small sum of money for general expenses. The *yeshivah bachurim* would turn over their notes to their *balebustes* who would use them to buy food for their boarders. The butcher stores and bakeries honored these notes as if they were real money.

Although my father had no official capacity in the *yeshivah*, he learned there constantly and often gave talks in the house to small groups of men and *bachurim*.

❦   ❦   ❦

I was past school age when I arrived in Mir and it was time for me to begin earning some money for the future. There was a Talmud Torah elementary school for young boys nearby. In the morning I taught seven-year-old boys the basics of *Chumash Beraishis* and some *Navi*. This school adequately filled the government requirements for education. The girls who went to the public schools did not have *limudei kodesh* during the day. In the evening the girls from very religious homes whose parents were concerned with this lack sent their children to special classes called *shiurei erev*. These evening sessions were held in the Talmud Torah building the boys used in the morning. The program consisted of only two classes made up of girls between the ages of eight and twelve. From five o'clock to seven o'clock each evening, I taught the eight- and nine-year-old girls *limudei kodesh* subjects such as *Tanach* and Jewish History.

❦   ❦   ❦

So passed the years in the *shtetl*. Day after day was occupied with living and learning, culminating in the "weekly *yom tov*" of Shabbos. Shabbos in the *shtetl* was similar to Bnei Brak today. The streets were filled with men and women dressed in their Shabbos best and the sounds of *zemiros* (songs) could be heard in the streets. Shabbos afternoon would be the time I usually spent with my friends. Often when they came to visit at my house, my father would take time from his learning to try to interest us in the *Midrash* on the *sedrah* so that we should not speak *lashon hara* (gossip).

Rosh Hashanah began the yearly cycle anew.

The *yeshivah* was filled to capacity on the *Yomim Noraim*, with hundreds of *bnei Torah* (G-d fearing men) pouring their hearts out to the *Ribbono Shel Olam*. The number of *bachurim* in proportion to the size of the city was amazing. Although there were three other *shuls* in the vicinity, the *yeshivah* was the one that seemed to actually vibrate with the intensity of the *tefillos*.

After Yom Kippur came preparations for Succos. People would build a *succah* for themselves or share one with several families. The *bachurim* would eat in their *balabuste's succah*.

Getting a *lulav* and *esrog* was an annual problem. They were extremely expensive and not easily obtainable. Each *shul* took upon itself to get one set of *arbah minim* (four species) for its congregation. The *gabbai* of the *shul*, or an emissary of his, would travel to a large city to buy the *minim*. The *yeshivah* would have several sets of *arbah minim* for the use of the *roshei yeshiva* and *bachurim*. After *davening*, the *gabbai* of the *shul* would give the *arbah minim* to a trusted young boy who would go from house to house to give the women and girls a chance to perform the *mitzvah*.

Succos is called *Zman Simchaseinu*, a time of our joy. In Mirrer Yeshiva it was literally that. Every night of *yom tov* the *yeshivah* vibrated with the celebration of *Simchas Bais Hashoeivah* (the celebration commemorating the water drawing ceremony in the Temple). *Simchas Torah* in the Mirrer Yeshiva was something special. The women would stand in a corner of the *bais medrash* separated from the men and wait excitedly for the *hakafos* to begin. Reb Yeruchem Levovitz stood in front. Behind him were the other *roshei yeshivah* holding the *sifrei Torah* lovingly in their hands. I vividly remember watching as Reb Yeruchem led the parade. He held two candles, one in each hand, and recited the *p'sukim* (passages) with intense concentration. His face glowed as he walked to the rhythm of the *tefillos*. Then the dancing erupted with all the life and excitement that is characteristic of young *b'nei Torah*.

Reb Yeruchem allowed each *hakafa* to last about an hour. When he felt it should end he raised his hand to signify its conclusion. Although the dancing was wildly exuberant, all action stopped immediately at a sign from the *mashgiach*.

Some of the men drank heavily to lift up their spirits and be able to dance with true *simcha* (joy). These *shikurim* were not violent or ugly. They truly made a *kiddush Hashem* with the love and joy of their dancing.

The snow would fall between Succos and Chanukah. A thick frosty white blanket covered the streets of Mir, turning the town into a winter wonderland. Travel was only possible by horse drawn sled, and the bitter cold often kept us indoors. However, the weather was brisk, exhilarating and often quite beautiful.

Chanukah was a joyous time and although the Polish winters were bitterly cold, the *menoros* warmed our hearts. Olive oil was very expensive and only the *roshei yeshivah* or the *rav* of a *shul* would use it, while the rest of us used regular Shabbos candles. Only the very rich had *menoros* made of silver. Most people had brass *menoros* and brass Shabbos *leichter* (candle holders).

After my father came home from *yeshivah* he'd light the *menorah* and we would sing. Everyone would then receive their Chanukah presents. They were not the lavish frivolous presents given today, but rather practical things. If one needed a pair of gloves or a sweater for the winter, Chanukah would be the time to receive them. To add to the festivities, all the children would be given a few pennies as *Chanukah gelt* to play *dreidel* or buy some candy with.

In my family, we had a unique *yom tov* that dates back approximately eleven generations. On *Rosh Chodesh Adar* (the first day of the month of Adar) we eat *Seudas Tosefos Yom Tov*, commemorating a miracle of long ago.

Rav Yom Tov Lipman Heller, author of a commentary on the *Mishnah* called the *Tosefos Yom Tov*, was the respected *Rav* of Prague. The government of Czechoslovakia delegated the job of collecting the Jewish community taxes to their leader, the *Tosefos Yom Tov*. The *Tosefos Yom Tov* imposed an income tax system by which he taxed the rich who could better afford it, more than the poor. The wealthy members of the *kehilla* (community) were angry that he "favored" the poor. They devised a plan to demote him from his rabbinical position. They went to high officials of the government and Church with their own translations of his previous writings. According to these versions it was easy to accuse the *Rav* of anti-Church and anti-monarchal sympathies, especially since these *goyim* were always more than willing to cooperate in getting a Jew into trouble. The *Tosefos Yom Tov* was immediately jailed, his properties confiscated and he was sentenced to death for treason.

At this time, his son Shmuel was returning home from *yeshivah* for a visit. As he passed a large open field, he heard a frightened cry.

Wheeling around, he saw a large vicious bull charging toward a small girl and her mother. Not wasting a moment, he slipped out of his coat, and waved it back and forth, trying to divert the bull's attention. By some miracle he managed to rescue the woman and child while emerging unscathed. As it turned out, Shmuel had saved the wife and daughter of the French ambassador to the King of Czechoslovakia. This high official was overcome with gratitude and offered to repay him in any way. Shying away from the praise showered upon him, the young *bachur* continued on his way.

When he reached home, he found his house wracked with grief; all his relatives and friends were crying in despair. After inquiring, he was told that his father had been imprisoned and his possessions confiscated. The young *bachur* immediately went to the prison to see his father. As they were talking he realized the *hashgachah pratis* in what had occurred earlier. The French ambassador now owed him a favor and perhaps he would intervene on his father's behalf.

After some high-level pleading and bargaining the *Tosefos Yom Tov* was released on the condition that he leave Czechoslovakia. Because this miracle occurred on *Rosh Chodesh Adar*, Rav Yom Tov Lipman Heller declared that all his descendants make this day a special *yom tov*. Over the years the tradition was lost to many families descending from him. However, in my family the *seudas Tosefos Yom Tov* has always been kept every *Rosh Chodesh Adar*. We set the table as if for Shabbos, with brightly lit candles, wine and special foods.

Purim was a time of great joy. Children accompanied their fathers to their close friends and relatives, to deliver *shalach manos*. The biggest treats to receive were oranges and chocolate. Oranges were very expensive and quite hard to get. When someone was sick, his family would spend a lot of money to buy oranges or grapes, for these fruits were said to give extra energy to a sick person. Purim was the only other time we received such treats.

We always had two *seudos*, one in the morning after *shacharis* and the next later in the day shortly before sunset. I remember a *d'var Torah* my father often told over at *seudas* Purim. Purim is a *yom tom* commemorating the salvation of *B'nei Yisrael* through hidden miracles. A common question asked is: What was the biggest of this series of miracles? My father always held that the appearance of Charvona was the biggest *nes* (miracle). He "happened to be" in the right place at the right time saying the right thing. We see from here the importance of *davar b'eeto mah tov* — saying the appropriate thing at the best time. Had Charvona said his piece a few minutes earlier, Achashveirosh might have been prepared for Esther's proclamation and dealt with it differently. Had Charvona spoken a few minutes later, the anger of Achashveirosh might have already slightly abated. His announcement was made precisely at the right time. We, too, must always recognize what to say to whom at a given time.

The layers of snow that had covered our sidewalks for months began to melt. We could see the sidewalks and streets we walked on. This all meant one thing — Pesach was coming. Pesach was not the expensive *yom tov* that it is regarded as today, but it did require a lot of work. We had two *matzah* baking factories where each family would go to bake their own *matzos*. Everyone baked large quantities of matzos because they were a major food for Pesach. Our wine was homemade. The raisins we received on Purim were collected and cooked to make raisin wine. My mother used to make some for us and some to sell to others as well, and in this way earned a little extra money that came in handy, especially at *yom tov* time.

With summer's arrival came *bein hazmanim* (intersession). Many families went to the country for these few weeks. It was healthy in the mountains with the fresh clear air, sunny skies, and the pleasant smell and shade provided by the pine trees. We stayed there only once but many families went annually.

By *Rosh Chodesh Elul* the city and the *yeshivah* were basically back to normal, for it was already time to prepare for the *Yomim Noraim*. The cycle continued.

A Shtetl Chassunah

everal years after our arrival, my father decided it was time for me to get married. He did not rely on *shadchanim* (matchmakers) for such an important matter but personally chose the *bachur* he wanted me to meet. His choice was Reb Ephraim Mordechai Ginsburg, a promising young *bachur* learning in Mirrer Yeshiva. We met seven times in my parents' house before becoming engaged. At that time young people did not go out on dates; they stayed in the house to

Our Wedding Picture

talk and get better acquainted. It was considered improper to be seen outside together before the engagement. However, once the engagement was finalized, the *chassan* and *kallah* (groom and bride) could walk together in public. Our engagement was a mere six weeks long.

Baruch Hashem I had no problem getting a wedding dress. To buy material and have a dress made to order was extremely expensive and we could ill afford it. However, several years before, Reb Moshe Shain and his young bride Ruchama moved to Mir from America. Over the years Ruchama became friendly with my sister and me. She had brought her *chassunah* dress from America and it fitted me perfectly.

A European wedding then was very different from one in America. Once, one of the *bachurim* brought back pictures of a relative's wedding in America. We were shocked when he told us that this was a *frum* Jewish wedding. It was held in a hall without separate seating and many of the women were not modestly dressed and did not cover their hair. It reaffirmed our belief that America must be a *treifa medinah* (country of impurity).

There were two ways to make a *chassunah* in the *shtetl*. One was on Friday afternoon, several hours before Shabbos. Then, a small smorgasbord was held before the ceremony for the entire town and only the friends and relatives were invited to the Shabbos meal that evening. My *chassunah* was different for it was held on a Tuesday afternoon. The *chassan's* father and sister came in from a nearby *shtetl* for the *simchah*. There was no such thing as holding a wedding in a fancy hall, nor in any hall for that matter. I was in a room in the *yeshivah* surrounded by my mother and all the other *shtetl* women, while the men were in a different room writing the *kesubah* (marriage contract). When it was time for the *badekin* (veiling) the women retreated behind me, and my *chassan* was led into the room by my father, his father and the rest of the men. After the *badekin* all the men immediately turned back to go to the *chupah* which was held outside in the street, as it is considered propitious for the wedding ceremony to take place under the stars. The men surrounded the *chassan* on one side of the street, while I was led outside to the opposite end of the block with the women around me.

The honor of accompanying the *chassan* and *kallah* to the *chupah* was given to two couples. These friends of the family were called *shusbaynin*. At my *chassunah* the *shushbaynin* were Reb Dovid and Batsheva Leshinsky and Reb Avrohom and Esther Mirel Kaplinsky. My mother and the other women followed shortly behind. The men stood behind the *chassan* while the women followed behind me as I walked towards the *chupah*. Rav Avrohom Tzvi Kamai, *Rav* of Mir, was our *mesader kiddushin* (officiating *rav*). After the *brachos* under the *chupah* were completed we were "danced" towards my parents' house.

Once we were inside there was a little dancing and singing before the main part of the *chassunah*, the *seudas mitzvah*. The women ate in one room, the men in another room, and a table for the poor

Mir: 1938 Newly married Rebbetzin Bender (far left) just moved to Mir. Standing with her are Yocheved Levenstein, Rivka Markowitz and Rebbetzin Ginzberg.

people was set up in the last room. It didn't matter that the meal wasn't lavish and that we were poor ourselves; when a *simchah* was celebrated, the poor were always invited. At my *chassunah* we had thirty *aniyim* (poor people). The women had gotten together to help cook and serve the meal. We did not spend the next several hours dancing to music; rather, we listened to all the illustrious speakers wish my husband and me *brachah* and *hatzlachah* in building a *bayis ne'eman b'Yisrael* (Jewish home). Then, of course, the *chassan* spoke, delivering a complicated *d'var Torah*.

Three days after my wedding my parents and sister left Mir for *Eretz Yisrael*. My father had been asked to be the *mashgiach* in the Lomze Yeshiva of Petach Tikva and there he stayed for three years. The death of Reb Yeruchem Levovitz brought my father back to Mir to fill the vacancy of *mashgiach*. However, our stay in Mir was to be coming to an end shortly thereafter.

Premonitions

he biggest surprise of World War II was Germany's role against the Jews. It had always been Poland, not Germany, that was notorious for its anti-Semitism.

I remember when World War I ended and the Russians left Poland. The German occupation lasted only a short time but my memories of it are far from unpleasant. After the boorish Russian rule we had been subjected to, the Germans were welcome. They were clean cut and kind, supplying us with all we needed. Their food packages consisted not only of staples but real chocolate as well, and they seemed genuinely concerned with our welfare. Their manners were impeccable and as a whole they were known to be fair. While Jewish students were barred from Polish universities, the German colleges welcomed them. Most occupations were open to Jews there as they are now in America.

Once, my family went to Germany for a visit. Being unfamiliar with the area we asked a German for directions. Most people would tell you to make a right and then a left, and then leave you to your own devices. This German, the epitome of politeness, escorted us to where we were headed. When he left, my father addressed us. "You probably think that the Germans are very nice people, right? I want you to know that if their government would so much crook its finger in the opposite direction and give them a license to kill whomever they pleased, they would shoot us in a minute!" This my father said almost two decades before the war. At that time it was inconceivable to many that a man like Hitler would rise to power in Germany. Life seemed as secure to the Jews in Germany as America seems secure to us today.

As the years progressed and Hitler's power increased, people still could not comprehend the possibility of a Holocaust happening in Germany and many Jews did not even apply for visas.

🦋 🦋 🦋

In Poland, life became harder and the hatred the *goyim* had for us was more apparent. We were afraid of the Polish government and instead of looking towards them for protection, we avoided as much contact with them as possible. The commandants, police chiefs, themselves were anti-Semitic. In Mir, the commandant Zavatsky did everything he could to bother us: issuing ridiculous laws, handing out summons for minuscule violations. We used to scold a child who refused to eat by saying, *"Ess Zavatsky koomt"* (eat, Zavatsky will come and get you).

Once, the Polish Senate passed a law against slaughtering of animals according to *halachah*, claiming it was inhumane. Meat was a staple in our diet and such a decree could not be lived with. Several *rabbanim* approached the government and, after much bargaining, had the decree removed. It was just another example of how the Polish people tried to make life difficult for us.

It is easy to see why we realized the danger of the situation before our brethren in Germany.

[On Thursday, August 24, 1939, Joachim von Ribbentrop, the German foreign minister, flew to Moscow to meet with the Russian foreign minister Viacheslav Molotov. The publicly known part of the agreement was that for the next ten years Russia and Germany would not attack each other. After the war, a secret document was found attached to the treaty. In it was the division of Poland between Germany and Russia. Germany was to take over the western parts of Poland while Russia would receive the eastern section. There was a special clause in the agreement regarding the city of Vilna and through this clause many *b'nei Torah* were saved.

In 1795 Poland lost her independence to Russia. Until 1918 Poland was divided among Germany, Austria and Russia. After World War I, when Poland regained her independence, she expected to repossess Vilna and its suburbs, for they had been hers from 1772 to 1795. However, since Lithuania had historical claims to Vilna dating much farther back than Poland, Russia gave Vilna back to Lithuania. Poland furiously refused to accept this and sent General Zeligovsky with an army to capture Vilna. After a short fight, Poland was able to integrate Vilna. The clause in the non-aggression pact between Russia and the Third Reich recognized Vilna as a city of Lithuania. This meant that it belonged neither to Russia nor to Germany and was officially a free zone.

On September 1, 1939, shortly after the signing of the non-aggression pact between Russia and Germany, Poland was invaded. The puny Polish army, lacking trained soldiers and adequate ammunition, was inevitably defeated by the Germans. Less than two weeks after the invasion, almost all of Poland was conquered.

Mir, however, was never under the German occupation. When the Third Reich had successfully conquered central Poland and most of its major cities, Russian troops non-violently moved into Mir. According to the von Ribbentrop-Molotov agreement, Germany was to take over the central and western sectors of Poland while Russia would receive the eastern part. Russia waited until Germany had subdued Poland so that they could claim their land without resistance. On *Tzom Gedalyah* (the fast of Gedalyah), 1939, the Red Army reached Mir. — Ed.]

Vilna's Miracle

s soon as the Russians arrived, we knew the *yeshivah* would be in danger. The Russians were preoccupied with their rampage through Poland, but we learned that they were preparing to exile us to Siberia for the "sin" of having a *yeshivah*. These plans were to go into effect when the trains were finished being used to transport the Polish goods they had stolen. We knew that we must leave Russian jurisdiction as soon as possible.

Shortly after *Simchas Torah* 1939, we learned that in two weeks Russia was going to transfer Vilna back to Lithuania. This act seemed strange to us then, since Lithuania had never even requested the annexation and Russia rarely gave anything away for free. Soon we saw their ulterior motive: to eventually use Vilna as a bargaining chip with Lithuania in forcing her to become communist.

During the weeks Vilna was in the process of being given over to Lithuania, it was possible to enter Vilna without a special permit, because officially Vilna was still under Russian rule. Lithuania did not have Russia's reputation for closing down *yeshivos* or persecuting religious Jews. My husband, like many others, decided to go to Vilna. We wanted to be sure we could raise our children in a *Yiddishe* environment with *yeshivos*.

My father and the other *roshei yeshivah* remained in Mir. They felt that the Russian takeover would not be permanent and eventually everyone would return to Mir. The *roshei yeshivah* wanted to make sure to be there when everyone returned.

Right after Succos my husband and I and my sister Yocheved packed our belongings and left Mir. We piled into a horse and wagon, bade goodbye to my parents, and were on our way. We boarded a long, terribly crowded train where people were practically on top of each other. My baby Esther began to cry and all my efforts to keep her quiet were to no avail. The others in our packed car began yelling at me, demanding why I had brought a baby on such a trip. Finally, after a seemingly endless three hours, we reached our destination.

Once in Vilna, we were told we could find accommodations in a privately owned basement. There we met twelve other refugees who had also taken up residence there. My husband and I were allotted one tiny room that barely held the two beds and baby carriage. All night my baby cried incessantly. I wheeled her back and forth over and over, hoping her crying would abate. The next morning the landlord told us we would have to leave because the other occupants had complained that her crying disturbed them. What could we do? We had nowhere else to go. I convinced him we could keep her quiet, if he would just let us stay a week. *Baruch Hashem* we found different, more pleasant living quarters by then.

In Vilna we met many people from *yeshivos* and towns all over Poland. Many had tragic stories of unsuccessful attempts to leave towns already occupied by Germans.

There was one horrifying story told to us by a man we met. He and his wife were traveling at night by horse and buggy along deserted dirt roads. The young couple sat up front by the reins while their three-month-old baby slept in the back. They traveled quietly, trying to sleep and avoid being noticed by patrols. Sunshine illuminated the sky as morning broke through the night. They were in Vilna when the young mother awoke. She realized with surprise that the baby had not cried all night. They pulled up to the side of the road and she went to check on her baby. Her heart sank lower and lower as she approached the back and saw a flap open. Frantically, she pulled out their belongings, searching, not quite accepting what must have happened. They had to face the fact that their three-month-old son had somehow fallen out the back during the night. They turned back down the path they came, searching the way they had traveled in hope of finding their child. It was all to no avail, and they returned to Vilna. That poor woman could not accept her baby's fate, that he had either died or had been picked up by *goyim*. She searched the face of every child of comparable age — questioning, hoping, could this be mine?

Rebbetzin Ginsburg with her sister in Keidon

After a while my husband saw that it was unlikely we would return to Mir because the war was getting worse. He sent an emergency telegram to my parents begging them to come to Vilna as soon as possible. Once the Lithuanian annexation would be official it would be very difficult to leave Mir. My parents and the other *roshei yeshivah* responded immediately and promptly joined us in Vilna.

Rav Kamai was the *Rav* of the town and he felt that as long as Jews would remain there, so would he. On June 27, 1941, the Germans captured Mir and within a few months executed most of the townspeople. We heard of this tragedy years later when we were on our way to America.

The Russian soldiers noticed the influx of Jews into Vilna but did not interfere for they, like everyone else, were waiting for the

Lithuanian government to take over. It was almost as if *Hashem* was holding up the show so that more *Yidden* could come in. The Lithuanian Army was late in coming, but that was for the best since after the official takeover, one could not enter Vilna without a permit unless he smuggled himself across the border.

Throughout all our travels the *yeshivah* continued on with their intense learning and *shmuessen* (lectures). Wherever we went, the *roshei yeshivah* would see to it that the *yeshivah* had a place to learn and conduct classes. That was always the number one priority.

The Lithuanian government set up a Refugee Department. This was to provide each of the thousands of refugees with a "Refugee Identification Card." The purpose was to insure that no refugee became a Lithuanian citizen. After several months, the Lithuanian government decided that the concentrated number of refugees should leave Vilna and should spread out in surrounding communities. In the beginning of *Teves*, two months after we had arrived in Vilna, the entire *yeshivah* moved to Keidon. It was a quiet, peaceful city in the middle of Lithuania but nevertheless, it was just another temporary stop in our journey to freedom.

❧ ❧ ❧

To sum up our situation: We were now in Lithuania, which was officially a self-governing country not involved in the World War. We knew the situation could not last and we must emigrate to a country out of the war zone. To travel out of a country one needs a passport and to enter another country a visa is necessary. Poland took away all citizenships, leaving us without a major requirement for obtaining a passport. Lithuania would not grant us citizenship and therefore we had to look elsewhere. We learned that in Kovno there was a Polish consulate under British protection. Britain was a member of the Allies and therefore recognized Poland's government-in-exile. The Polish consulate was supposed to help the Polish citizens in exile. There we received certification in lieu of a passport. The certificate was just a piece of paper on which was printed the words: "An exchange for a Passport — Representatives of Poland in Kovno." Although these passports were issued by a government that did not exist, these documents eventually enabled us to emigrate.

Although we now had valid passports, we still had to get visas. After Shavuos 1940, as a result of pressure from the Russians,

Lithuania set up a Communist government. We recognized this as the beginning of the end of independent Lithuania. As a last hope we turned to, and found help from, an unexpected source. Shortly before the establishment of the Communist government, Sigi Haara, a Japanese consul, opened his headquarters in Kovno. This in itself testified to Divine Providence. Never before had Japan had more than one consul in Lithuania. Suddenly the consul sent an emissary to Kovno for no apparent reason — and it was to this representative that we appealed to.

He offered us what is known as a transit visa, admitting us to Japan as a stopover to the country to which we were actually headed. The problem with the transit visa was that it was still necessary to obtain a visa to another country, a final destination.

The government of Holland had an island called Curacao. In order to encourage people to settle there, it issued permission to anyone who wanted to go there regardless of whether or not they had a visa. We approached the Dutch consul for visas to Curacao because, although we never intended to go there, such visas would make us eligible for the Japanese transit visas. However, since anyone could enter this island without a visa, the consul did not have a visa to give us. We asked the consul to put in writing that we did not require visas to enter the island. The visas we purchases stated: "The bearer is permitted to enter Curacao without a visa according to Dutch regulations." We paid the Dutch consul and headed back to the Japanese consul to obtain transit visas.

Although he was well aware that we never intended to settle in Curacao, the Japanese consul agreed to give us transit visas. We were charged an extremely low price of two *lits* per person (equivalent to fifty cents in those days), one fourth of what we paid for the so called Curacao visas. The transit visas were stamped: "Good for transit through Japan to the island of Curacao and other Dutch islands." This consul was so helpful to us he would stay in his office after closing time to sign the visas and even granted transit visas to those who could not procure the Curacao visas. As soon as Russia took over Lithuania, all consulates in Kovno were ordered to close. Sigi Haara endangered his life by signing all the visas he could during the next three weeks, prior to his departure.

❀ ❀ ❀

My father received a certificate to emigrate to *Eretz Yisrael* while we were in Keidon. He never even considered taking advantage of it for that would have meant deserting the *yeshivah*.

Several days before the Russian annexation of Lithuania the Communist regime ordered the *yeshivah* in Keidon to disband.

The *yeshivah* separated into three groups and settled in nearby villages. My family and I went to the village of Shat. During the time the *yeshivah* was spread out my father walked through mud and snow, often endangering his health, to deliver his *shmuessen* in the nearby villages where the *yeshivah* was dispersed. This kept the *yeshivah* unified in spirit although we were separated.

❈ ❈ ❈

In September of 1940 the NKVD bureau in Lithuania opened two emigration offices, one in Kovno and another in Vilna. This in itself showed tremendous Divine Providence, for Russia as a rule did not allow emigration. It seems that the Russians established these offices specifically to get rid of the numerous Jewish refugees from Lithuania. Surprisingly enough not only did they not exile us to Siberia for being "refugee traitors" and wanting to leave Russia, they treated us fairly well.

Around the beginning of *Teves* our exit permits were approved. For two weeks names of those granted approval were posted on the bulletin board at the NKVD offices. The Emigration Department existed only until the end of that winter and those who did not take advantage of the opportunity had to stay in Russia. Most of the Jews who had to stay in Russia were later sent to Siberia.

Now that we had our emigration permits, passports and visas, we needed only to buy tickets in order to leave. We planned to take a local train from Kovno to Moscow and then get the Trans-Siberian train to Vladivostok. From there we could find a ship to sail to Japan. The only available place to procure tickets to Vladivostok was the Intourist office in Kovno. Intourist is Russia's official department of tourism. When we approached the office we were shocked to find that they would charge us the same amount Americans paid — one hundred and seventy American dollars per person. We asked them where we could obtain American dollars when owning them in Russia was illegal. The officials replied, "We do not care," and hinted that we try the black market.

We now had a tremendous problem. The *yeshivah* had to produce fifty thousand dollars to cover the purchase of tickets for the *bachurim*, *rebbeim* and their families. Fifty thousand dollars then was the equivalent of a half a million dollars today. Besides the enormous amount of money we needed, we were also restricted by time, for our exit permits would expire after six weeks. We urgently wired Reb Avrohom Kalmanovitz, the director of the *yeshivah* in New York, to tell him of the situation. He immediately called a meeting of *rabbanim*, relatives and students in New York. There he explained the danger we were in and how only immediate financial aid could help us. From that meeting alone forty thousand dollars was raised. The additional ten thousand dollars needed was secured by Reb Kalmanovitz through loans. Through the aid of devoted people, Reb Kalmanovitz was able to secretly send us the money. It was cabled to Intourist of Kovno payable to the Yeshiva of Mir. We received the money approximately two weeks after we had requested it. Now that we had our tickets we were on our way.

Leaving Russia

e all left together, *roshei yeshivah*, *rebbeim* and their families along with about three hundred *bachurim*. A tour bus took us from Kovno to Moscow on a trip that lasted all day.

Before we were allowed to enter Russia proper, we had to pass through customs. Back in Mir I had been able to secure some American money via the black market. American dollars were very valuable because the United states economy was fairly stable then. In Poland it was legal to have foreign currency, though hard to obtain; in Russia it was illegal to carry American money. When we reached Kovno I had one twenty-dollar bill that I guarded carefully. Before going through customs I sewed the money into the shoulder pads of a dress and packed it into the suitcase. We waited on line for our turn to be inspected by the government official. Instead of taking my husband and me together, they took him into a room I was terrified that they would find the money and send my husband to Siberia. The minutes ticked by and the tears streamed down my cheeks as I tried to control my emotions and fears. My parents were behind me but they didn't understand why I was so upset, for I hadn't told them of the money we were trying to smuggle. An old friend of the family came over to me and tried to calm me down, asking what was wrong. As quietly as I could I whispered to him the reason for my tears. With a horrified look he walked away quickly, afraid to be considered an accomplice. Finally my husband emerged from the room, white, shaken but *Baruch Hashem* safe.

This twenty-dollar bill we risked so much for, I was able to save for a while. However, in Japan there was a young man with financial problems. I lent him the money then, and years later, when we arrived in America, he paid me back.

We were treated as any tourist on a trip through Russia would be treated. Our lodgings were at an expensive hotel with beautiful rooms complete with a private bath, phone and constant heat. We had no problem with kosher food for we were able to order oranges, and other fruits and kosher sardines from Poland. While we were at the hotel we were offered sightseeing tours in Moscow at the museum, the zoological gardens, etc. This was all included in our ticket, free of charge.

With all our first-class accommodations and VIP treatment, we were just very thankful to *Hashem* when we were left in peace. In each room there was a bug recording every word we said and any word spoken that could be interpreted as a slur against the government could put us in jail immediately.

After spending a few days in Moscow, the Trans-Siberian railroad arrived and we boarded it for Vladivostok. The trip took three weeks with the train stopping only briefly and occasionally for fuel. At such stops my husband would leave the train to go out and buy some food for us. I would stand by the train's exit and nervously await for him to return. Sometimes they would announce that the train was departing shortly. My eyes searched the streets anxiously lest he miss the departure. *Baruch Hashem* this never happened but I never felt safe throughout that journey.

For three weeks our diet consisted of a piece of Swiss cheese and bread for breakfast and a piece of salami and bread for supper. One redeeming factor of the journey was being comfortable. The coaches were heated so that although the temperature outside was as low as fifty or sixty degrees below zero, we were warm.

During the trip my husband was afflicted with a terrible toothache. We had forgotten to bring along aspirin and I had no medicine to help relieve his pain. There was one man among us who had a small supply of aspirin. His wife, the poor woman, could think only of survival, and insisted that he give away none of his precious cargo. But *Baruch Hashem*, the man had pity and gave some to my husband. It was a hard time, we were scared and never felt safe or secure.

On the Vladivostok train we were constantly apprehensive. Every day the conductors went through each car to check that we had the proper papers. We shared a car with Reb Baruch Sorotzkin and his wife. Somehow, they had not been able to get very good papers. Even at a cursory glance, one could spot that they were forgeries. In such a situation one would think that they would constantly be nervous and scared. This was not the case. The only manner in which I ever saw Reb Baruch was engaged in learning. From the time I awoke until the time I went to sleep, I never saw his eyes wander from the *Gemara* in his lap, his wife at his side. When the officer entered the car, his eyes did not blink. He flashed his papers for a split-second inspection, never stopping his learning. The amazing thing was that the conductor never asked to examine their papers and they arrived safely in Japan.

We waited in Vladivostok for several days, until the steamship arrived to take us to Japan. Before we were allowed to leave Russia for Japan, we were searched again. This time each person was inspected from top to bottom, every article of clothing. Although they found nothing illegal they made sure to profit anyway. My sister and I both had beautiful rings made for us by a cousin of ours who was a jeweler in Warsaw. These rings were taken from us.

All through our trip we were "escorted" by officials of the NKVD. We were not left alone for a minute until we passed the Russian border. It was only then that we could really breathe easily since throughout the journey we could never be sure the Russians would not change their minds about letting us out of the country.

Japan

he freight steamer that was to take us to Japan was small and old. The Japanese sea in the winter is usually quite rough, and this year was no exception. The small, dilapidated boat did nothing to ease the discomfort. I was terribly seasick during the several days of the journey and *Baruch Hashem*, my husband was strong and could take care.

We arrived from the bitter Russian frost to experience the pleasurable Japanese spring weather. The city of Kobe was absolutely beautiful. Its combination of mountains, seas and pure fresh air was like paradise to us. All year the climate there is pleasant, but that spring was even more special. The trees were blossoming, the sun was shining, and we were out of Russia.

Life in Japan, even for so short a time, was not easy. We were housed in a gigantic apartment house. Each family was entitled to one room, so a three-room apartment had three families living in it. There was one bathroom for the entire building and it was inconveniently situated on the top floor.

Food was scarce and sugar almost unobtainable. Sugar is a good energy source since it contains so many calories in a small amount. I had two weak parents, a sick sister and a baby to care for. I knew they needed sugar to keep their strength up, so I worked hard to get some. It was a full-day trip on an old-fashioned, dilapidated streetcar. I had to travel from one end of town to the other to a small discreet grocery store. Sugar was rationed and it was illegal to try to obtain more than one's quota. I approached the salesgirl in back of the store and begged her to sell me a few kilos of sugar. *Baruch Hashem* my trips were not usually in vain, and I was able to buy at least a little sugar.

Our transit visas in Japan were valid only for ten days and the *yeshivah* administration was constantly appealing for extensions. We received help in this quarter from a Japanese professor who was very influential in government circles, partly due to his royal heritage. Dr. Kotsuji was a professor of Semitic languages at Tokyo University. He came to Kobe to see the *yeshivah* and learn about us by observation. His visit made such an indelible mark on him that eighteen years later he converted to Judaism, becoming Avrohom ben Avrohom.

During our stay in Japan my husband received a certificate of entry to *Eretz Yisrael*. The Brisker Rav declared responsibility for my husband, myself and our daughter if the Israeli government would grant us entry permits. Had we accepted the certificates we would not have had to go through Shanghai and might have spent those years in a much easier manner. My husband, however, did not even consider leaving my parents, who were old and frail, or deserting the *yeshivah* at such a time. We therefore went on together with the *yeshivah*.

Time was passing and we still did not have entry visas for the United States. When the Japanese realized that we had little chance of emigrating, they ordered us to go to Shanghai, an international city in China. By the end of August, 1941, we were out of Japan.

Shanghai

[After the Opium War between Britain and China in 1843, several nations obtained territorial rights and privileges in China. The city was split into five zones with each country ruling its own section. England and Holland ruled the international zone while the United States, Japan, France and China had their own zones. To enter Shanghai, one had to receive a permit from either of the countries and this certification permitted one to go anywhere within the city. In 1937, Japan conquered Shanghai when they invaded China. However, Japan did not interfere with the governing of the city and it retained much of its international status.

The Jewish community of Shanghai was made up of several groups of emigrés. A very small community was started a few hundred years before by Jews from the East but it was not until about twenty years before World War II that the community was really developed. It was then that Ashkenazic Jews emigrated to Shanghai in large numbers and eventually became moderately wealthy. In 1938, about twenty thousand Jewish refugees from Austria and Germany were exiled to Shanghai by the Nazis. At the time this seemed tragic, but eventually this proved to save their lives. The refugees from Japan received a lot of help from the community there. In fact, just as in Japan, when they left after the war the entire Jewish community followed them to other western countries. — Ed.]

apan expelled us to their zone Honka. The *Sephardishe* community, outside the Japanese zone in the international quarter, was led by Rav Meir Ashkenazi. They had a large and beautiful *shul* known as the Bais Aaron Shul. The *yeshivah* took over this building, using it for classes, lectures and constant learning.

For those living in Shanghai during those crucial war years it was doubtless easier than for those who had to endure Russian prison camps, German concentration camps or other such situations. However, it was still an extremely difficult and unpleasant time. The men and *bachurim* were able to throw themselves into their learning and find solace there. We women were left at home with not much to do other than care for the children, shop for food and worry about our husbands and fathers. We were strangers in a foreign land. The people looked strangely different, spoke an unintelligible language and the city itself was unpleasant.

In the city, contagious and dangerous diseases were rampant. People were inflicted with black boils, leprosy, cholera, dysentery and typhus. I remember walking down streets lined with bodies burning with fever from leprosy. These remnants of humanity were taken out to the streets so that the people in their homes would not become infected. The Japanese authorities in Honka assembled the dead in the middle of the streets and piled them on trucks to be taken to isolated areas for the people were too poor to afford funerals. Frequently, when we went out of our zone to go shopping, we would see the curbs lined with corpses that had not yet been collected.

When one of my sons was two months old, I contracted a case of typhus. I refused to be hospitalized because I wanted to be home to take care of my newborn child. The doctor came to the house to treat me whenever he could. I never fully recovered and throughout our stay I was weak, my resistance low. After the birth of my third son I became anemic. For weeks I was terribly weak, had no appetite and was coughing terribly. My cough developed into bronchitis and I was put into the hospital.

There were several *bachurim* sick with typhus. A Lubliner *bachur* used to come to the hospital to be *mevaker cholim* (visit the sick) and he would always include me in his rounds. It was always uplifting to have visitors and it was terribly tragic when he contracted the awful disease and never recovered.

❦ ❦ ❦

On December 7, 1941, after the bombing of Pearl Harbor, America declared war on Japan. American and British troops were evacuated from the city as Japan tightened their military security. They strictly censored all mail, especially letters from an enemy country such as the United States. All our monetary transactions had to be conducted secretly through neutral countries. Any and all contact with America was illegal. The threat of death hung over our heads, for that was the automatic punishment for treasonous communications.

Baruch Hashem, we were able to establish contact with Rabbi Kalmanovitz in America. This was done through neutral countries such as Sweden, Switzerland. Argentina and Uruguay.

Another avenue used to procure funds was directly from Switzerland. Mrs. Recha Sternbuch, hearing of our plight, formed an organization called the HJEFS, *Hilfsverein fur Judische Fluchtlinge in Shanghai* (Relief Association for Jewish Refugees in Shanghai). She made appeals, arranged for the transport of funds and helped us immeasurably.

❧ ❧ ❧

In the ghetto we had little contact with the *goyim*. The Chinese were a backward people who lived under filthy, primitive conditions. They were not very educated and communication, when necessary, was difficult. We would go to the market in groups of several women. There we would embark on our mission: to purchase the food we needed. This was no simple task. The Chinese knew only their native tongue and although many of us knew several European languages, Chinese was not one of them. With wild gesticulations and creative sign-language we managed to bargain successfully. This was the extent of our communication.

Our accommodations in the ghetto were cramped and crowded. Each family, regardless of size, was allotted one room. When we first arrived, my husband and I had only one daughter but by the time we left, *Hashem* blessed us with three more children.

We divided our room with a curtain. In one third of the room my husband and I slept, and the remaining walls were lined with beds. This left little space to move. Our "spacious" hall outside was the community kitchen where all the housewives in the apartment house assembled to cook.

The *yeshivah* where my husband spent his day learning was outside the ghetto. He left for *Shacharis* at seven o'clock in the morning returning late at night just before the ghetto would close. All day I used to worry as to whether he got there safely, without being accosted by soldiers, and whether he'd return home safely. It was finally at night when I saw him approaching from the window that I was able to breathe freely. When I became sick my husband came home earlier in the afternoon. He used to learn at home while caring for the small children.

Every family received an allowance from the *yeshivah* for food and clothing. From the few dollars received, I would lay one aside to be saved for the future. Although it usually meant scrimping to get by, it helped considerably when we arrived in America.

One of the greatest pleasures we had was receiving a package from America. Each package afforded different treats such as chocolate, rice cooked with pineapple, and even meat. My husband never let us eat the food immediately. First we read all the ingredients, ascertaining that the shortening was okay and that any questionable additive was negligible.

Upon arriving in Shanghai, several *bachurim* from the *yeshivah* married girls from among the German and Russian refugee families. Boys who had lost their entire families in Europe began to build families of their own. In my family, we experienced our own private *simchah*. My sister Yocheved married my husband's brother, Reb Reuvein Ginsburg. Their wedding was celebrated with all the excitement and *kedushah* (holiness) of my own *chassunah* in Poland not long before.

※　※　※

In April of 1945, World War II came to an unofficial end with the capitulation of Germany. Japan's surrender in August would make this end final. Those six months between the downfall of Germany and that of Japan were very dangerous for us.

Shanghai, being under Japanese rule, was a prime target in American bombings. In order to provoke a Japanese surrender and finally end the war, America intensified its bombing of Shanghai. There were several air raid shelters in Honka. Ours was in an old movie house. Our whole building would crowd inside, *davening* that the bombs would not hit anyone.

I remember one evening when we were told to expect heavy bombing of our section. I gathered together my three young children and my infant, and fled with my mother and sister to the shelter of the movie house. Together we huddled fearfully as we listened to the sounds of the bombs destroying everything around. When the danger abated we emerged from the shelter to return home. The block next to the building we lived in was a burned-out shell and we learned later that thirty people had perished. Our block was almost totally intact.

[At the end of the summer of 1945 the American navy was coming closer to the beaches of Shanghai. The threat of invasion was imminent, not just from the Americans but from the Chinese Nationals, led by Chiang Kai-shek, as well. The Japanese army in Shanghai was preparing for war. They maintained that they would fight for Shanghai to the very last man. — Ed.]

On August 9, 1945, the first atom bomb was dropped. Three days later the second one made the Japanese surrender. This happened before an invasion could take place and Shanghai was conquered without a battle. After the Japanese surrender, the Chinese Nationals occupied the city without a shot being fired.

Now that the war was over we wanted to travel on to settle somewhere permanently. Exit visas arrived and we all lined up to get them. Everyone was excited but nervous — excited that we were finally leaving, but nervous that enough visas might not be granted. As I was standing on line, I notices a familiar sight. A conscientious Mirrer *bachur* (now a prominent *rosh yeshivah*), was standing at his *shtender* (lectern) — his *shtender* from Mir that he had taken with him through all our travels — learning from a *Gemara* while waiting on line. The nervousness of the crowd did not affect him, the commotion around him never stopped his learning.

I walked over to him and said, "If I had a daughter of the right age, I would want you to be her *chassan*. Someone with your *hasmodah* (diligence) and *bitachon* (trust) is the kind of husband I would want for a daughter of mine."

❦   ❦   ❦

All we needed now were entry visas to the countries we wished to emigrate to. Rabbi Kalmanovitz, with the help of the Vaad Hatzalah, worked tirelessly to get us these visas. Each person wishing to emigrate had to have someone sponsor his coming to America. The sponsor would guarantee that the immigrant would not be a hindrance to society. After arranging for sponsors for each and every one of us, Rabbi Kalmanovitz now had to bring us to America. Every available ship was being used to bring home American soldiers abroad. As a result of a lot of bargaining and exhausting effort he arranged for visas, sponsors and a big ship. In January of 1947 we were on our way.

America

Our three week ocean voyage was marked by sea sickness and difficulty. I was ill most of the time. My husband took care of the children and some of the healthy *bachurim* lent their help. Reb Shmuel Berenbaum, present *rosh yeshivah* of the Mirrer Yeshiva of Brooklyn, was a young *bachur* at the time. In one hand he held the *sefer* he was learning from while the other held my baby son. He kept the baby quiet and content throughout the journey.

We arrived in San Francisco in late January. There we spent a very pleasant six weeks. Although our quarters were cramped, not more than a room per family, the weather was beautiful and therefore our accommodations seemed pleasant. Most of the Jews living there were not *frum*, and I don't even recollect a major *shul*. We stayed there long enough to recuperate from our ordeal, but were eager to arrive in New York. There we could permanently establish the *yeshivah* and settle ourselves with other *Yidden*.

From San Francisco to Rockaway we traveled by train. Although the *yeshivah* was in Rockaway only until Pesach my family and I stayed there for the summer. Again, we had only a small cramped basement with little comfort, but Rockaway had the boardwalk and beach which aptly compensated. It was more pleasant than a burning New York summer could be.

Shortly before the *yomim tovim* we moved to East New York where we lived in a rented apartment not far from the *yeshivah*.

Picture the situation I was in. I was a thirty-two-year-old mother of, *b'li ayin hara*, five children. We were strangers in a foreign country. I had always loved to read, secular literature as well as Jewish, and now I could not even read the notes my daughter brought home from grade school. Such a situation I could not accept. Although I did not have the advantage or opportunity of attending school, I was determined to remedy my illiteracy. Every time I received a note from school I would go down to the landlady who would read and explain to me what it said. I would then study it and repeat the words over and over, matching the word to the characters on paper. I sat down and worked on my children's homework with them. I advanced with them until I too could read,

City Hall, 1946, a kaballas panim for the yeshivah organized by R' Kalmanovitz

write and comprehend the English language.

Several years after we settled in New York, my parents along with my sister and brother-in-law decided to move to *Eretz Yisrael*. Mirrer Yeshiva was firmly established in New York and my father felt it was time for him to join the *yeshivah* in *Eretz Yisrael*. It was a sad and tearful parting for I had never been far from my family. However, my husband felt our place was in America and it was here that we stayed.

Rebbetzin
Sara Baila Kaplan

> " *This was the extent of my childhood travels. Bad transportation made every trip a burden. However, we also had less of a need to get away. Life was quieter, more geshmack. We didn't have many luxuries or riches, but we didn't feel we needed them, either.* "

Rebbetzin Sara Baila Kaplan was born in Novardok. While still a child she moved to Baranovitch, where her father, Rabbi Tzvi Hirsch Gutman, became a *mashgiach* in Rabbi Elchonon Wasserman's famed *yeshivah*. In Baranovitch she married Rabbi Mendel Kaplan, an outstanding *bachur* in the *yeshivah*.

The Kaplans spent the war years in Vilna, Japan and Shanghai. After the war Reb Mendel became a *rosh yeshivah* in Bais Medrash L'Torah in Skokie, Illinois. Several years later Rabbi Kaplan became a *rosh yeshivah* in Talmudical Yeshivah of Philadelphia, teaching until his passing two years ago. Rebbetzin Kaplan currently lives in New York.

Personalities of Baranovitch

he *yeshivah* in Baranovitch was legendary. Its beginnings stem from a little known story involving my mother-in-law, Esther Kaplan. One afternoon when she was at the market place shopping, she happened upon R' Chaimke the Sofer. R' Chaimke was a pious learned *tzadik* who spent most of his days writing *sifrei Torah*. [Reb Mendel Kaplan used to tell over this incident illustrating the greatness of Reb Chaim Sofer. The Chafetz Chaim was passing through Baranovitch by train. When the train stopped at the station the entire town lined up to catch a glimpse of him. The Chafetz Chaim, however, did not move to the window in order to be seen. "But," he remarked to his *shammas*, if R' Chaikel (meaning R' Chaim Sofer) is outside, I would definitely go over to the window to see him." So great did the Chafetz Chaim regard R' Chaim Sofer. — Ed.]

"R' Chaimke," my mother-in-law addressed him, "why do you spend your time writing *sifrei Torah*? You should be creating *leibedige sifrei Torah*! Open a *yeshivah*."

"Esther Kaplan, how can I open a *yeshivah* without money?" he replied sadly.

The ideas and possibilities already started churning in her head. "Don't worry, I'll help," she promised. She started by going around the neighborhood and finding people to sponsor a *bachur* by providing him with one major meal each day. By implementing the *teg* system, she eliminated a portion of their food expense. Other arrangements were made with the butcher and the baker to supply bread and meat for breakfast and lunch.

During the first World War, food was very scarce. People would go out to the fields to dig for potatoes, eating even those not ripe. One day Esther Kaplan met R' Chaimke walking, a sack slung over his shoulders, obviously on his way to dig potatoes. "If *you* are going out to dig for potatoes for yourself, what will become of the *yeshivah*?" she exclaimed.

"What else can I do?" he replied despondently.

"Go to all the people who have supported the *yeshivah* until now and get a little from each one. Use what you get for yourself and the *yeshivah*. Collecting money for them is far more befitting a man of your caliber than digging for potatoes," she answered. And that was what he did.

As the *yeshivah* grew, they decided that it was necessary to hire another *rosh yeshivah*. R' Elchonon Wasserman, already recognized as a brilliant scholar, was the first choice. With his arrival, the *yeshivah* expanded. Half of R' Elchonon's house was used for him and his family while the other half became the *Bais Medrash*. In the kitchen they began to cook meals for the *bachurim* to supplement the *teg* system.

✿ ✿ ✿

We lived across the street from R' Elchonon and became very close to him and his wife. Early in the morning we used to run to the window to watch as he walked out of his house. People would turn around to stare at his face because of his radiance, his *hadras panim*. Everyone was in awe of him.

He was the personality who led the *yeshivah* morally and physically. Aside from his *shiurim* and brilliance in Torah, he personally raised funds for the *yeshivah*. There were times when he was away from the *yeshivah* for months, raising money in places as far away as America.

Often, the *yeshivah* received meat or other foods on credit with the understanding that the bills would be paid when the funds were available. After a long, hard journey from America, R' Elchonon arrived in Baranovitch late at night. Six o'clock the next morning the butcher heard a knock at his door. He went to see who was at his house so early in the morning. You can imagine his surprise when he saw R' Elchonon standing there.

"*Rebbe* . . .?!" he stammered. "I . . . we didn't even know you had returned from America. What is the matter?"

"*Baruch Hashem*, my trip was successful and I've come to pay the bill," Reb Elchonon answered.

"But *Rebbe*, after arriving in town so late, why did you come here so early? Just as I've trusted you to pay until now, I could have waited several more hours?!?!"

"Before, I did not have the money to pay and had no choice but to buy on credit. However, when I arrived last night in Baranovitch, I did have the money. I couldn't disturb you late at night, so I waited until early morning and immediately came to pay you back. If at all possible one should never leave a debt unpaid, even for the shortest amount of time." With that, R' Elchonon left.

❧ ❧ ❧

Reb Yisrael Yankev Lubchansky became the *mashgiach* of the *yeshivah*. Every Shabbos, between *Mincha* and *Maariv*, he gave a *shiur hisorirus* to the entire *yeshivah*. His speeches were so uplifting, inspiring and lofty that we girls wanted to hear them also. We used to stand beneath an open window of the *Bais Medrash* and strain to listen to his words.

Living in the house of R' Yisrael Yankev was a very special friend of mine, Vichna Eisen. She and her brother had been orphaned at a young age and came to live in their uncle's house. She was a lively girl and a wonderful student.

Word reached us in Baranovitch that far away in Cracow there was a wonderful woman, a Frau Schneirer, who was starting a school of higher learning for Jewish girls. To Vichna this was the epitome of everything she wanted: a place where she could not only satisfy her intellectual desires but where she could do so among *frum* girls like herself.

The problem was that she needed a high-school diploma in order to be admitted. The only high school in Baranovitch was a public school and R' Yisrael Yankev refused to let his niece attend such a school. Vichna was heartbroken as she saw the castles she had built in her dreams crumbling down. Undaunted, she wrote to Frau Schneirer asking why she needed a secular diploma to attend a Jewish school. The reply stated this was the only way to narrow down the many applicants to the seminary. However, for a girl with such a determination to learn she, Frau Schneirer, would make an exception. All she would need was proof that she had passed five high school classes. After privately taking these lessons, she was accepted to Bais Yaakov Seminary in Cracow and after she left, we rarely saw her. However, none of us would ever forget that bright and lively girl whose determination turned her dreams into reality. [Vichna Eisen later married Rabbi Baruch Kaplan. See page 214. — Ed.]

Growing Up In Baranovitch

he first few years of my life we lived in my birthplace, Novardok. My sister and I were taught to read *Aleph-Bais* by a tutor, a *yungerman* just out of *yeshivah*. When I was still a small child, we moved to Baranovitch where my father became a *mashgiach* in the *yeshivah*.

My father was a very special person who dedicated his life to learning and to guiding those who wanted to learn. He knew how to handle the *bachurim* with wisdom and not anger. Every night between *Mincha* and *Maariv* there was a *mussar seder* in the *yeshivah*. As is usual in a *yeshivah*, some *bachurim* listened, some slept, and some talked. One night as my father was quietly making his rounds, he saw three *bachurim* sitting near each other. One was dozing and the two other were whispering to each other. He walked by them but didn't say a word while the *mussar seder* was in progress. A short time later he saw the three of them together. He began to talk to the one that had been sleeping about the conversation of the other two. The *bachur* looked at him blankly.

"Well, if you hadn't been sleeping you would have heard what your friends were talking about," my father said pointedly.

My father felt it was very important for girls to learn *beur tefillah*, the translation of daily prayers. *Gemara* was totally off limits, and even *Tanach* wasn't absolutely recommended for teaching to girls. Therefore, the best thing for girls to learn was the translation of *tefillos*. Not only could one learn a great many lessons from the words of our *chachamim* but it also gave our *tefillos* extra meaning.

Aside from learning with our father, my sister and I had very little education. We attended a public elementary school for a number of years. Although the students were mostly Jewish, the teachers were Polish and no Jewish subjects were taught. We learned a few *limudei kodesh* subjects with a tutor whenever a large enough group of girls or the teachers was available.

❦ ❦ ❦

Baranovitch was a peaceful town. We had very little contact with *goyim* and those we did meet were not outwardly anti-Semites. It

Rabbi Tzvi Hirsch Gutman

wasn't until shortly before the war that they began to show their true colors.

Compared to other Lithuanian or Polish towns, Baranovitch was quite large. During the summer months, we went out of town for a vacation. Once on our way to the mountains, we stopped off in Mir. I remember how incredulous we were at the size of the city. This town which was spoken of with awe by all *Yidden* could fit into one corner of Baranovitch!

We spent about three days in Mir, taking advantage of the time to visit my brothers in *yeshivah*. During that time I had the *zechus* to meet the great *mashgiach*, Reb Yeruchem Levovitz. His pure *tzidkus* (righteousness) made an indelible *roshem* (impression) on me.

The only other times I traveled out of Baranovitch was to visit a doctor in Vilna. Baranovitch had few doctors and no specialists in the city or nearby. Vilna was the home of several well-known doctors, and it was there that people went for special problems. My adenoids were infected and I had to travel to Vilna to get them removed.

In the *yeshivah* world at that time, Vilna was synonymous with its *Rav*, R' Chaim Ozer Grodzenski. I went there to ask for a *brachah* and to send regards from my father. During my visit in Vilna I was to stay with R' Shlomo Heinman, a special friend of the family. I was not sure how to get there from the house of R' Chaim Ozer and I asked him for directions. His clear directions led me straight there.

Five years later I had to return to Vilna to get my tonsils removed. Again I stopped off at R' Chaim Ozer's house for a *brachah* and to relay my father's regards. I was not satisfied with the doctor I had used five years before. I asked R' Chaim Ozer if he could recommend a new doctor for me. After giving me several names he inquired, "By the way, were you able to find your way to R' Shlomo Heinman's house with the directions I gave you?"

This was the extent of my travels. Bad transportation made every trip a burden. However we also had less of a need to "get away." Life was quieter, more *geshmack*. We didn't have many luxuries or riches, but we didn't feel we needed them either.

⚘ ⚘ ⚘

Our house was situated near a train station. Day and night people came off the train hungry and tired, in need of a place to stay. When it was still early in the evening my parents would prepare us for bed saying, "*Kinderlach* (children), go to sleep. People might need a place to stay and we will need your pillows, "*chap arein*," use them now." Many times we woke up to find our heads lying on the hard bed, our pillows being used by a weary traveler.

My mother was a great *tzadekes*. Her concern for people extended far beyond what we regard as normal. On *Shabbos* we were allowed to carry because there was a kosher *eruv*. After we ate the *Shabbos* meal, instead of lying down for a nap, my mother went from house to house collecting any leftover *challah*. There were no preservatives, and the *challah* would spoil if it was left out for a long time. So she collected the *challah* while it was still fresh, and went out and gave it to the poor. This was how she spent a good part of her *Shabbos* afternoon. *Erev* Yom Kippur she didn't bother to eat herself, but went out to collect food to distribute to *aniyim*.

When the older Gutman girl left for Eretz Yisrael, she and her friends posed for this picture. She is on the bottom left. Above her is Rebbetzin Sara Baila Kaplan. To the right of Rebbetzin Sara Baila Kaplan is Rebbetzin Vichna Kaplan.

She ignored her needs out of her concern for others.

She and my father both hoped I'd be able to attend Bais Yaakov of Cracow. However, my mother became ill when I became of age and I stayed home to help. I was only a teen-ager when she was *niftar*. The loss was painful not only for me but for the entire town as well. Everyone recognized that we had lost a *tzadekes* of rare caliber. On the day of her *petirah* every store in Baranovitch was closed out of *kavod l'meis* (honor for the deceased).

❀ ❀ ❀

After the death of my mother, I ran the house and became a teacher. For several years I taught various grades ranging from kindergarten to third grade.

The time came when I was of age to get married. A few years before, Reb Elchonon suggested a shidduch for my older sister. The boy lived in *Eretz Yisrael* and she had never seen him. Nevertheless she agreed to the *shidduch* on Reb Elchonon's recommendation. She left for *Eretz Yisrael* in 1928 and never returned home.

Once again my father approached R' Elchonon and asked him to recommend a *bachur* as a *shidduch* for his daughter. R' Elchonon immediately said, "R' Mendel Kaplan is the one."

From the time he was a young *bachur*, R' Mendel surpassed many of his elders in his breadth of Torah knowledge. Every morning he had a *seder* (learning schedule) with R' Elchonon himself, working with him to prepare that day's *shiur*.

R' Mendel was a native of Baranovitch and our families were quite close. His sisters were friends of mine and I was at their house often. The possibility of the *shidduch* did not occur to any of us until R' Elchonon suggested it. Besides being very young to be contemplating marriage, R' Mendel was also a year younger than me. However, after hearing all his attributes from R' Elchonon, my father decided it was an excellent *shidduch*. At first the age factor bothered me a little but my father felt this was of no consequence. Since parents always have the best interests of their children at heart, and children are too young to know what's best for them anyway, I listened to my father and agreed to talk with the *bachur*. R' Mendel came to the house a few times to talk with me and my father. After several visits the *shidduch* was settled and preparations for the *chassunah* began.

On the day of my *chassunah* there was a terrible snowstorm. The *chupah* took place outside in the frigid cold. Regardless of the bad weather, R' Elchonon was dancing under the *chupah* in order to be *misame'ach chassan v'kallah* (bring joy to the new couple).

After the *chupah* everyone went home to prepare for *Shabbos*. That Friday night after *Maariv* (evening prayers) all our friends and relatives were invited to our house for the Shabbos meal and *sheva brachos*.

For the next few years we lived near my father in Baranovitch. My husband learned in the *kollel* and, when R' Elchonon was away, he said R' Elchonon's *shiur*.

The Outbreak Of World War Two

hortly before the outbreak of World War II a decree was made by the Polish government prohibiting kosher *shechitah* (slaughter), claiming that it was an "inhumane" form of slaughter. The government made sure to supply all the stores with ample amounts of non-kosher meat, hoping that the Jews would eventually buy it. For over a month all the Jews of Baranovitch, *frum* and non-*frum* alike, boycotted the stores. It was at this time that R' Elchonon said, "As long as this strike lasts, that is how long Poland will last."

Well, the decree lasted barely a month, and Poland lasted not much longer. With the signing of the non-aggression pact between Russia and Germany, the two countries began to carve up Poland. The Russians stormed into Baranovitch, creating mixed feelings among the residents.

Like Poland's other *yeshivos*, we felt we must leave Russian jurisdiction. Russia was known to be intolerant of *yeshivos* and we were afraid of what they might do to us. The businessmen of Baranovitch did not share our fears. They felt that Russian occupation would not be permanent and would not really affect them. Those who stayed were either deported to Siberia or perished in the hands of the Germans when they later broke the non-aggression pact.

We decided to escape to Vilna, as many other *yeshivos* did. [See Rebbetzin Ginsburg's interview — Ed.] As soon as we could, we boarded trains to Vilna and began our eight-hour trip. As soon as we arrived, we faced the problem of finding apartments. We moved to a town within Vilna called Semelitia and tried to settle down.

❦   ❦   ❦

The Lithuanian *goyim* were terrible anti-Semites. They took advantage of every opportunity to make trouble for us. One Friday afternoon, on a day which happened to be a Christian holiday, my husband was outside chopping wood for Shabbos. Suddenly he sensed a presence behind him.

"What do you think you are doing here?" demanded a large menacing man.

"I'm chopping trees for firewood," my husband said calmly.

"What do you need so much firewood for?" he returned.

"Tomorrow is our Sabbath and we are not allowed to do any work then," answered my husband.

"Tomorrow might be your holiday but today we have a holiday. How dare you desecrate our holiday by doing menial work?!?!"

The *goy* was outraged. He brought several government officers and demanded that they arrest my husband for his conduct. My husband was held in the courthouse while they decided what his punishment would be. I was waiting at home, frantic for word of the situation.

While he was in the courthouse, a man he knew came in. When he heard what had happened, he explained the situation to the authorities, convincing them that they would gain nothing by sending a scholar to Siberia. After several hours they released him. That Shabbos we had an extra *simchah* to celebrate.

The year passed slowly. We came just after Succos and by the time Shavuos came around we were fully prepared to leave. Finally, we received our transit visas and were on our way to Japan.

❁ ❁ ❁

Many people leaving Vilna could not procure proper legal papers. They had to have false papers forged for them. The Shulberger Rav had papers that were bad forgeries. As he went through customs we were very nervous that his papers would be spotted as forgeries. The officer spent several minutes examining his papers. Handing the papers back, the officer said softly, "I am going to let you through. However, you must get better papers because these forgeries are going to be spotted."

None of us had any idea why this *goyishe* officer let him through, but we saw *hashgachas Hashem* clearly. Throughout our journeys, through Japan, Shanghai and finally, America, we saw how *Hashem* helped and guided us.

America

e sailed from Shanghai to America in January 1946. The boat landed in San Francisco after three weeks of traveling. San Francisco was the most beautiful place I had ever seen. The weather was sunny and pleasant, trees and flowers in full bloom. After the awful atmosphere and accommodations we had in Shanghai, San Francisco was wonderful. We stayed in a hotel for two days, before continuing our journey.

My husband's brother lived in Chicago. He sent train tickets for the whole family to join him there. The train was like none we had been on. It was beautiful and spacious, with room for us to sleep comfortably. Shortly after our arrival my husband became a *rosh*

yeshivah in the Chicago *yeshivah*, Bais Medrash L'Torah, which was later moved to Skokie. The *frum* Jewish community of Chicago was very small at the time. There were no adequate schools for girls or for boys. We sent our son to Telz Yeshiva in Cleveland when he was very young, just ten years old. When the girls reached high school age, we felt they could only receive a proper education in a Bais Yaakov, and we sent them to New York. At that time the journey was long and expensive which meant they could come home only for *yomim tovim*. We kept them in New York at great expense while my husband earned only sixty dollars per week. This was very difficult for us and after some years we moved to New York and my husband became a *rebbe* in the Talmudical Yeshiva of Philadelphia.

Rebbetzin
Judith Grunfeld

"
And so it was decided: I was going to (the Bais Yaakov Seminary in) Poland. I went out and bought a new coat and hat, took my briefcase with my notes and the commentaries of Hirsch, and set out. I got into the train, unaware that the step off the platform was a step into history.
"

Rebbetzin Judith Rosenbaum-Grunfeld was born in Hungary, but moved to Frankfort, Germany, while still an infant. From early youth, her ambition was to teach Jewish children, and she took extensive training in education.

On the advice of Moreinu Rav Yaakov Rosenheim, Miss Rosenbaum traveled to Poland to help teach in the new educational endeavor begun by Sarah Schneirer. She spent several years in the fledgling Bais Yaakov Seminary, gaining renown as an educator.

She returned to Germany in 1929, and shortly thereafter married Rabbi Dr. Isidore Grunfeld. In the early 1930's the Grunfelds, sensing the danger of the growing Nazi power, fled to England, where Rebbetzin Grunfeld continued a distinguished career as educator and authoress. Her husband, *Dayan* Grunfeld, wrote many important books, among them translations into English of the works of R' Shamshon Rafael Hirsch, including *Chorev*. *Dayan* Grunfeld was *niftar* in 1975.

Growing Up in Frankfort

 was born in Budapest, Hungary, my father's native land. When I was about a year old the family moved to Frankfort on the Main, Germany, the country where my mother's family lived. She stemmed from a renowned German rabbinic family, the Bambergers. Her grandfather was the famous Wurtzberger Rav and her father was a prominent *rav*. His wife, my grandmother, lived with utmost righteousness and modesty, a true *tzadekes*.

My father was a Hungarian *talmid chacham* who learned in Pressburg. The Hungarian background of his family was characterized by a warm, easygoing, often informal atmosphere. My parents felt that the German Jewish community would be a better setting to raise children. There, the attitude was more conscientious, reliable and exacting. Children were provided with a solid education, stressing the importance of diligence, accuracy and scholastic achievement. I still feel that this attitude was more valuable than any other I have encountered either then or now.

Life there was pleasant. The people of Frankfort were generally wealthy and much of their money helped support religious needs within and outside the community. The *shuls* were big and beautiful, with plenty of *sifrei Torah* and *seforim*. In addition, the community founded an excellent Jewish school system for boys and for girls.

From the time I turned six until the age of sixteen I attended Hirsch *Realschule* (elementary and high school). The Orthodox German Community was a product of Rabbi Shamshon Rafael Hirsch's perspective, characterized by the words, *Torah im derech eretz*. My school, like the community, functioned strictly along the lines set by R' Hirsch.

The teachers as well as the administration were all *frum* and most of the pupils came from fine Orthodox families. Dr. Gerson Lange, the headmaster, was not merely an educated scholar, but a G-d fearing, pious man who was a *lamdan* as well. It was said that at four o'clock every morning he walked to the other side of town, a very long way, to learn with his brother.

All things considered, one might expect such a school to have an intensive Jewish curriculum. But we had only one class of Jewish studies each day. This was because we did not have the partition between Jewish and secular studies that exists today. All our secular studies were taught with the view that everything in the world is a product of *Hashem's* wisdom. There was no concept of Torah being Jewish and all other subjects *goyish*.

Our *chachamim* teach that witnessing the birth of a baby can make someone believe in G-d. Look at the power the close observation of nature can have on a person's belief! By studying the miracles of nature we can fully comprehend *Hashem's* greatness. This is how we studied the sciences.

We studied botany: how a tiny seed is planted, germinates in the ground and becomes a large, strong tree. Each species of a plant, tree, grass and herb has its own function and use. Look at G-d's wisdom in the way He provides for every creature.

We studied biology, the intricacies of *Hashem's* creation. Look how *Hashem* created our bodies. If we cut our skin we do not have to glue or staple it together, for it heals itself.

Mathematics is a phenomenon in itself. The world was created so that all mathematical precepts apply down to the smallest detail. Can one deny that there is a Divine presence behind it? Practically speaking, we could not function in this world as Jews without knowledge of mathematics. We need it for daily actions, to build a house, a ship, a plane or even a *mikvah* (ritualarium). The knowledge is essential not only in mundane matters, but to fulfill *mitzvos* (precepts) as well.

The way we learned our secular subjects obliterated the line between secular and Jewish study. Therefore, one period of strictly Jewish learning a day meant more than it means today. In that one session we did not cover a lot, but what we learned was remembered. I was lucky, for the teacher I had for my last several years of schooling was an excellent one. Every one of my contemporaries remembers until today the things that she taught us. She made us memorize important lessons, and kept us interested. Miss Jentiller Jeidel — as she was called — became engaged and, although we were happy for her, we were upset that she would no longer teach us.

In our Hebrew classes we learned *Chumash*, *Pirkei Avos* and sometimes a little *Tehillim*. We did not learn the primary commentaries such as Rashi or Ramban, but rather concentrated thoroughly on R' Hirsch's commentary.

The school was housed in two large buildings connected on every floor by a hall. Dr. Lange went from the boys' building to the girls' side through the halls. Both buildings held ten classes of approximately thirty pupils each.

❦ ❦ ❦

I graduated after ten years of schooling and looked forward to furthering my education. My dream was to become a fully trained teacher, able to fill young Jewish minds with knowledge.

Yet an obstacle blocked my way. There were only two Jewish seminaries in Germany, neither in my town. As much as I wanted to reach my goal, my parents and I agreed, my place was at home. Therefore, I decided to attend the nearby non-Jewish seminary to complete my education.

Shortly after I began I was faced with a dilemma. At that time, the concept of a five-day work week was unheard of. Saturday was considered a weekday no different than Monday or Tuesday, and regular classes were scheduled. Other *frum* girls attending the seminary went to these classes on Shabbos. They did not carry or write, but just listened. They were not actually desecrating the Shabbos, and yet it was *uvdah d'chol*, something done during the week that is not proper to be done on Shabbos, much like reading a newspaper or secular novel — acts not forbidden *per se* — but which should not be done on Shabbos.

Class attendance was a criteria for graduation and I could not just absent myself. Therefore, I wrote a letter to the government requesting to be exempt from Saturday classes. A short while later I was granted my request. I saw clearly how, whenever we try to do something right and good, *Hashem* helps.

During those years at school, I learned a lot and received a strong foundation to build upon. Yet I never had a feeling of being a part of the seminary, never a feeling of belonging although I was always friendly, inquiring after a classmate's health or offering a pencil to one in need. They, too, made friendly, polite overtures, but even after several years I still felt like a stranger. Outwardly I never showed it, inwardly I felt it.

Sometimes we had school outings for three or four days. Helen, the only other *frum* girl in our class, and I prepared sandwiches of cheese or sausage in advance. In the evenings, when the class went to the canteen for supper, we went back to our sleeping quarters in the youth hostel and ate our own kosher meals. One evening after eating, we rejoined our classmates as usual. A classmate had several plums and offered us some of the luscious fruit. Then she stopped herself and said, "Oh, I am sorry! I forgot you do not eat in the evenings." She thought we never ate with the group at the canteen because our religion forbade us to eat in the evening. She did not realize that we separated ourselves to eat our prepared food. Although we spent so much time together, my classmates were virtually ignorant of Jewish customs and laws. We melted into the crowd, our "strange" ways ignored but tolerated.

The seminary headmaster was a fine gentile, a learned and kind man. One day he approached me and began to talk of school and other related matters. In the course of conversation he asked curiously, "Why do you skip Saturday classes? I know other religious girls come to classes, why not you?" Thoughts raced through my head as I tried to think of a satisfactory answer I could give him, without giving the other girls a bad name. I decided to appeal to the scholar in him. "Well," I answered, "you are right. I could attend classes without transgressing my laws, but we have such a rich Jewish literature, a treasury of books and commentaries on the Five Books of Moses, that I like to devote at least one day a week to explore these houses of knowledge." The subject was thereupon closed.

I attended seminary classes for three years. During the fourth year we were required to student-teach under supervision. There was a German elementary school attached to the seminary and it was there that we gave our model lessons.

When the year finally ended, I was relieved and excited that I would soon have the opportunity to open young Jewish minds, my real goal.

During my seminary years I was involved in a Jewish youth organization known as the Ezra. It was an Orthodox organization for extracurricular activities. I was assigned a group of young girls to lead. Every Shabbos we got together, played games, sang songs and said *divrei Torah*. We, the leaders, had a lot of influence over these girls. The atmosphere was one of fun and learning in the realm of Torah. It was, in a sense, a forerunner of the Bnos groups of today.

Sent on a Mission

was twenty when I graduated from the four-year seminary with a teaching degree. From there I went to the university to earn my doctorate in education.

One day I received a telephone call from the Hirsch school from which I had graduated. A teacher was ill — could I come in to substitute? I had a few weeks' vacation between terms at the university and I agreed to spend them teaching at my alma mater.

For those few weeks I threw myself into my job. It was Chanukah time and I wanted to make a party for my class. At that time it was not the custom to use class time for such "frivolity" as socializing by means of parties; school was for learning and parties were for fun. However, I felt the best way to teach children the joy and happiness of a *yom tov* was to have them experience it personally.

I approached the new headmaster and received permission for my revolutionary endeavor. For the next few days I put my heart and soul into preparations for the party. We had some lemonade, chocolate and other treats. I made up a poem about Chanukah, telling my students the miraculous events in an entertaining way. We sang songs and had a wonderful time.

The next morning, as I walked through the halls, I saw the headmaster approaching from the opposite direction. As we passed, I said, "Good morning, sir." He stopped in his tracks, looking at me sternly. "There is still an orange peel on the floor," he said, pointing to the incriminating evidence.

I could not believe what I was hearing. Here I had gone and thrown my whole soul into making a memorable party for my students and all he could comment on was the one remaining orange peel. He did not ask how the party was, whether it was a success or whether the children enjoyed it. Nor did he congratulate me on a job well done or at least recognize my efforts. The orange peel on the floor was more important than the eternal light of Chanukah reflecting in the hearts of the children.

I bent down, picked up the peel, and none too graciously apologized for the "mess." As I walked to my class I thought to myself: This is not the place for me. To teach in such a school, lacking the warmth of teaching, was not what I wished to do. At four o'clock, when I finished my lessons, I left the school and went directly to Moreinu Harav Dr. Rosenheim.

Rav Rosenheim was a recognized Torah personality. He traveled widely to Poland and Lithuania and other parts of the world to give support and assistance, educating and helping institutions. I knew him very well because his daughter was my best friend and nearly every day I had spent some time there doing homework and visiting.

Usually, there were people waiting to talk to Rav Rosenheim about their problems. I was practically a member of their household, so I walked directly into his office where I found him. He was sitting in his study, books all around him.

"Rabbi Rosenheim," I began, "I would like to teach in *Eretz Yisrael*. There I can accomplish something worthwhile. Do you know anything about *chinuch* there, or the situation of the schools ... Do you think there is a place for me?"

"Not in *Eretz Yisrael*," he said decisively. "I know where you should go. You should go to Poland."

"Poland?"

"Yes. I have seen a woman there who has hundreds of children with her. On her own, she attempts to educate and care for as many children as possible. However, she cannot manage all by herself and trains young girls, some not more than twelve years old, to assist her as teachers. This is a place that needs you."

"No thank you, Rabbi Rosenheim," I answered. I left quickly, turning the preposterous suggestion over in my mind. Go to Poland? Ridiculous! Poland was the land of poverty. Men came from Poland to Germany to collect money to marry off their daughters or support their families. I recalled an unfortunate Jew from that country whom my father had brought home one Friday night. His bedraggled appearance, the way he hungrily ate his food, his black handkerchief that kept dipping into his soup did nothing to improve my impression of the country. Poland was a place we looked down upon as being backwards, less cultured and less advanced. People visited London or Paris, but who ever visited Poland?

"Why are you so late?" my mother asked me, when I returned home.

"I stopped by to talk to Rav Rosenheim," I replied. "He advised me to go to Poland to teach."

"Go to Poland?" exclaimed my mother. "Out of the question."

So the issue was settled. I did not want to go, my mother did not want me to go, so I would not go.

Providence, however, did not concur.

Three days later I received a letter:

> Dear Miss Rosenbaum:
>
> We are very happy to hear you are coming to Poland. We are expecting you to stay with us for two months to help us to set in action our educational program. Please get your passport ready and your papers in order.
>
> Thank you,
> Dr. Leo Deutschlander

Immediately I wrote my reply:

> Dear Sir:
>
> I have not agreed to go to Poland. I am too young, inexperienced and unprepared to go. I have not accomplished enough and do not feel equal to the task you want me to undertake. Thank you for your offer, but I am sorry, I cannot accept.
>
> Sincerely,
> J. Rosenbaum

A few days later the next letter came:

> Dear Miss Rosenbaum:
> ... You'll find a ticket enclosed. The train will leave ...
> Dr. Leo Deutschlander

The letter had a sort of hypnotic power, beckoning me to its destination. I have warned them that I am not good enough, I said to myself, but they sent me this ticket anyway. I still have several weeks of vacation. If I go one of two things will happen — either I will have a pleasant time or an unpleasant time. If I have an unpleasant time it will be for a short while and will soon be over. If I have a pleasant time it will be a worthwhile experience. Either way, I have little to lose.

I decided to talk to my parents.

"Let me risk it," I said. "They cannot say I do not know enough because I told them that already. If it does not work out it is their fault, not mine."

And so it was decided: I was going to Poland. I went out and bought a new coat and hat, took my briefcase with my notes and the commentaries of R' Hirsch, and set out. I got into the train, unaware that the step off the platform was a step into history.

The Bais Yaakov Years

 traveled alone, a tedious journey of many hours, until I arrived in Cracow. I was told that I would be met at the train station. If no one was there to meet me I was to go to the Hotel Royal, where a room was reserved in my name.

When I stepped off the train I looked around for a Jewish face, but to no avail. Obviously something had happened, and no one was going to appear to greet me.

I took some money out of my purse and approached the Polish porter. Unfortunately I could not speak his language so I showed him my money and said, "Hotel Royal". Somehow we communicated. He took me to the hotel and stayed with me as I rang the bell to get in. It was pitch dark, two o'clock in the morning, and everyone, including the hall porter, was asleep. For several minutes we stood there ringing the bell, waiting for an answer. Finally a man came sleepily to the door.

"Rosenbaum?" I said hopefully.

He took me upstairs to my room. I was thrilled to see a nice bed, with some water on the table to wash. Exhausted, I said *Shema* and immediately went to sleep.

The next morning I awoke to a knock on the door.

"We are from the Agudah. We are to accompany you to the station, from where you will travel further to Novytok," they said. "There the girls will be waiting."

"What if they are not there?" I asked.

"If not, here is the address."

"Colonia Bais Yaakov, Robov," I read.

When I got to the station at Novytok, there was nobody there. Again I took out my money and began to look for someone to help me. Sure enough a Pole soon came by, driving a haycart.

"Colonia Bais Yaakov?" I said, motioning to him that I would like

Outdoor classes

a ride.

There I was, dressed in my new hat and coat, holding my smart briefcase, on the back of a horse-drawn cart with mounds of hay as my seat. Where am I going? I thought. We did not pass any towns, only seemingly endless forests.

Finally, finally, I saw a woman in the distance. She was a faraway figure in a long gray dress, surrounded by girls on all sides. They saw me and started running, exclaiming, *"Die fraulein fun Deutschland"* (the young lady from Germany). Their excitement was contagious, as swarms of girls lifted me out of the cart towards Sarah Schneirer. My belongings were taken, the driver was paid and I was seated in the shade of a tree listening to Sarah Schneirer telling me her story.

The next morning my work began. The first few days were strange and bewildering. Four Western-trained teachers, myself included, had come to join, meet and teach girls from a totally different upbringing. We could only hope that our world and the chassidic world of these girls would blend and not clash.

Any fear and tension were soon dispelled. The Western teachers were Dr. E. Ehrentreau, who was then *dayan* in Baden, a city near Vienna; Miss Rosalie Mannes of Zurich; myself; and of course Dr. Deutschlander. The Polish girls were, for the first time, meeting teachers who were Torah-true university graduates, who taught by the principles of Rabbi Shamshon Rafael Hirsch and his students. The bringing together of these two worlds was a risky experiment that only succeeded through the extraordinary capabilities, tact, warmth and diplomacy of Dr. Deutschlander. He was able to dispel the natural reserve between us and build up confidence in each other. He made us feel united by common goals and aspirations.

I threw myself into the job at hand, giving every ounce of energy, knowledge and feeling that I possessed. I would stay up most of the night preparing lessons. Often I would write nonstop until three o'clock in the morning, when I would finally take a rest. I would lay in bed, my book clutched in my hand, catching a few minutes of sleep. At five o'clock in the morning I would wake up, regretting the lost time and eager to return to my preparation. A few hours later I taught those very lessons.

I was fortunate; *Hakadosh Baruch Hu* helped me to give over that which I did know. I was able to present concepts, ideas, things I had already learned and make them meaningful to these girls. I drew knowledge and inspiration from the commentary of R' Shamshon Rafael Hirsch. Of other commentaries I did not know much, but perhaps it was better that way. Everything was taught along the same lines, each lesson adding to the other, forming a complete building.

The girls became enamored with the lessons. They drank in the words, the knowledge. Torah became more than just a book for men in *yeshivah*; it was a way of life that enlightens and fascinates in its beauty and wisdom. They had never had such interesting and stimulating lessons. To them, until now Torah meant more restrictions: "You must not go to movies," "You must not wear nice dresses if they are cut out a bit," "You must not eat this", "You must not do that" . . . They were never told the positive side, that the whole world rests on the Torah, the perfection of a life of Torah.

Their upbringing was so different from the way we were brought up in Germany. In our world there was a lot less of a distinction between the boys' upbringing and the girls'.

The *chassidim* educated their sons in *yeshivos*, but kept their daughters ignorant, while we educated both the boys and the girls. While the boys learned *Gemara* and *mishnayos*, we girls were taught *Chumash*. When the boys went to *shul* on Shabbos, we girls

Leading calisthenics

also went. This is why Sarah Schneirer needed educators from Germany. We had something to give over to these girls.

I did not know much, but what I knew I could present with warmth, feeling and enjoyment. We did not just lecture, we made the school days lively with a song, game or joke. We translated *deracheha darchei noam* through actions, showing that G-d's ways are pleasant, righteous and enjoyable. We can also be happy, we can also dance, we can also be young and we can see the beauty of Torah in everything.

When I came, I brought a bit of youthful action along. Although Sarah Schneirer was not old, she was not young in her ways. She was the pure soul behind all our actions, but I was the young friend, the confidante. I was able to relate to them and they to me. When Friday night came, I showed them that it was a time to dress a little nicer, brush one's hair a little fancier and that this, in honor of Shabbos, was not only allowed but preferable. They needed to know that the desire to look nice and feel good can be acceptable within the sphere of Torah.

So I was in Robov for six weeks, teaching on the meadow, sitting on the grass, learning in a pleasant, country atmosphere. Morning calisthenics, *davening*, eating, learning were all done together in that unique *heimishe* environment. We went for walks together, sang together and played together. There was a friendship and

Judith Rosenbaum, affectionately called "Fraulein Doctor"

comradeship for girls who had never had such harmonious camaraderie before.

These six weeks in Robov marked a revolutionary breakthrough. Never before had girls joined together, united in learning, in learning to unite. This marked the first organized educational program of the Bais Yaakov movement. It was the foundation to build upon.

After those weeks it was time to depart. "Oh, you will come back," everyone said. I merely smiled, thinking to myself, I am never going to come again. I was grateful for the experience. I loved the girls, loved those weeks of teaching. However, I had worked so hard, given so much, that I felt drained, like a gas tank on empty. I had lost so much sleep, I felt it would take at least a year to regain those lost hours. The lessons I gave encompassed all the material I had ever learned or heard and my store of knowledge was now empty.

I went home and resumed my studies at the university. However, I did not forget those weeks in Robov. I told everyone I met about Sarah Schneirer, her work, her dream and her accomplishments this

below. One of the girls ran to the window and saw a carriage stop in front of the school. Running from the room she called over her shoulder: "Frau Schneirer, Frau Schneirer." Fifty, sixty, seventy girls echoed her call. They threw their pens down and pushed their books aside in their rush to get outside. They all crowded around the carriage as Frau Schneirer was led, almost carried into the building. The mood of the school turned to one of unmatched excitement. Although she had just traveled and lectured through the night, perhaps several nights, Frau Schneirer, who always had time for her girls, immediately narrated her experiences of the journey. She spoke of her trip with a mixture of seriousness and amusement. Later, every girl turned back to her work, as if there had been no interruption. Still, one could sense their happiness in having listened to Sarah Schneirer's report on her travels.

We did all we could to enforce the idea that *Yiddishkeit* was not just a mass of restrictions, but an ideal way of life. I decided to organize an outing for the girls. We left the school with rucksacks on our backs and walking sticks in our hands. For four days we started out early in the morning, *davened* and hiked through the woods. Every so often we stopped to eat and to say *divrei Torah*, and at night we slept in a youth hostel. We had a wonderful time.

Shabbos was always beautiful in the seminary. We sat in a large dining room crowded with tables and chairs. Sarah Schneirer made *Kiddush* and delicious, traditional Shabbos food was served. In between courses and *zemiros*, girls and teachers stood up and delivered *divrei Torah*. I even wrote home to my father and friends to ask for original *divrei Torah* I could give over, when I ran out of material. After each girl gave over her piece of Torah, as if with one voice we sang out, with that girl's name: "...*haht gezugt a Torah — gezugt a Torah ... haht gezugt a Torah — gezugt a Torah* (said a Torah message)!"

Every *yom tov* was special, as *yom tov* is. However, for fun and jollity, Purim was outstanding. The girls dressed up, mimicking us in funny, entertaining skits. Rebbetzin Wachtfogel, presently a teacher in Bais Yaakov Seminary, was a pupil at the time and she borrowed my jumper and skirt and acted my part. We gave each other *Shalach Manos*, enjoying the *yom tov* immensely.

There are certain days in the year that, though they are special, are often overlooked. Sarah Scheneirer made these days into special events, setting a precedent for her students. The day before *Rosh*

Chodesh is *Yom Kippur Kattan*. Our *chachamim* teach that it should be used as a day of penance. In Bais Yaakov of Cracow it was a special day spent in a special and memorable way.

Sarah Schneirer, followed by one hundred and twenty girls, would walk to the Rama's Shul in the Cracow ghetto. The Rama was Rabbi Moshe Isserlis, author of the *Mapah*, which incorporates his dissenting rulings into the *Shulchan Aruch*, and this *shul* was named after him. After everyone had *davened* there, we walked to the graves of such *gedolei Yisrael* as the Rama, the Bach (Reb Yoel Surkis) and the Tosefos Yom Tov (R' Yom Tov Lipman Heller). Our *Tehillim* in hand, we assembled around the tombstones. The atmosphere of *kedushah* and tranquility around the graves of *tzaddikim* inspired the young girls.

Lag B'Omer is the Rama's *yahrzeit*, the anniversary of the day of his death. Hundreds of *chassidim* filled the cemetery. This atmosphere of holiness and reverence for *gedolei Yisrael* made a profound impression on Sarah Schneirer's students. It was as if Jewish history was alive and unfolding before our eyes. When the girls went home they felt that their footsteps on the cobbled streets of the Cracow ghetto echoed the footsteps of these great and holy men. It made them determined to make sure that this echo would resound in the future.

❧   ❧   ❧

It was 1925 and I was to go home soon. Before returning I wanted to take advantage of being in Poland to observe first-hand an example of *chassidishe* life. I had never encountered any actual *chassidim* and, in meeting girls from such backgrounds, my curiosity was stirred.

Two of my pupils lived in Gur Kavarja, the Ger community. It was *selichos* night when I boarded the train bound for Ger. The majority of my fellow passengers were *chassidim* traveling to join their *Rebbe* for the *Yomim Noraim*. I sat in the back, a solitary young girl. They probably thought I was a Polish gentile, a young woman with uncovered hair!

At the station Rosa Rosa and Esther Rosa, two sisters whom I had taught, came to greet me. They brought me directly from the station to the Gerrer Rebbetzin. She welcomed me with a friendly smile. I could just make out the sound of *selichos* being chanted in the nearby *Bais Medrash*. Quietly, I walked around the building to a window and stood with my nose against the pane to watch. I had never seen anything quite like this! They were crying and pouring their hearts out with an intensity and fervor that was like a spiritual blaze.

The next day, I had an audience with the Gerrer Rebbe himself. He stood at one side of the room, and I at the other, with a kind of counter separating us. I was lucky enough to get a *brachah* for myself and my parents from such a great *tzaddik*. Before I left, Rebbetzin Chaya Alter, the wife of Rabbi Betzalel Alter, the Gerrer Rebbe's brother, gave me a *mussar sefer* with a personal inscription. This I have in my cherished possession still today. Everyone was wonderfully warm and friendly to me throughout my stay.

Not long after I returned to the seminary, word reached Sarah Schneirer that the Bobover Rebbe disapproved of her Bais Yaakov. She decided that she wanted to find out what his reservations were; to try and convince him of her pure intentions. Many warned her that even if she was determined to go she should not attempt to go during *Yom Tov*. Because of the Rebbe's opposition to Bais Yaakov, she might not be able to find a place to spend *Yom Tov*. They would probably not invite her. When I heard she was actually going to Bobov I told her that I wished to accompany her. I wanted to see and experience these walks of Jewish life.

We left *erev* Succos, contrary to all advice, traveling the distance by train. From the station we walked into town to find lodgings at a nearby boarding house. After we had settled ourselves in, we lost no time in going to the house of the Bobover Rebbe to introduce ourselves. The Rebbetzin kindly invited us to join them for all the *yom tov* meals. That night we dressed in our *yom tov* best and went to eat in the Bobover Rebbe's home. They had two *succos*, one for the men and another for the women. In our *succah* sat the Rebbetzin, her six daughters, Sarah Schneirer and myself. There was a large table with all the plates, cups and gleaming silverware piled in the middle. I asked my hostess if I could set the table for her. "No," she replied, "we do not set our table with individual settings."

"Why not?" I inquired.

"Well," she answered, "when you set a table for thirty people, and for some reason you have thirty-one guests, one person feels left out. By not setting for an exact amount of people you avoid the problem of hurting anyone's feelings and can still have unexpected guests." Her kindness and consideration for others remains impressed in my mind.

Yom Tov was warm and enjoyable. We spent most of our time with the family of the Bobover Rebbe, becoming close with his Rebbetzin and daughters. On *Chol Hamoed*, in celebration of *Simchas Beis Hashoeivah*, the *chassidim* gathered in the *shul*. They danced with excitement and happiness as the *Rebbe* himself played the violin. I remember the *"leibedig"* singing, dancing and music of that night until today.

I was able to approach the *Rebbe motzei Yom Tov*. I gave him three *Kvittlach* (request of a blessing): one requesting a blessing for myself, another for my parents and a third for the success of Bais Yaakov. He gave the blessing to myself and my parents and was then silent. I felt I had to know why he would not give his blessing to Bais Yaakov. I summoned up the courage and asked him. He answered cryptically, "Bais Yaakov should have *siatah d'shmayah*, help from *Hashem*. His fears were that, by mixing girls from so many different backgrounds, they would tend to keep the easy customs and ways of some while abandoning the strictures of others. He felt such a mixture of varied backgrounds was dangerous. The bad should become good but the good should not become bad.

I must mention that as they realized the advantages of Bais Yaakov the Bobov community accepted it. Today the Bobover Rebbe's daughters are heads of Bais Yaakov in London and his grand-daughters are products of a Bais Yaakov education.

❦ ❦ ❦

During my years in Bais Yaakov I rarely went home. Bais Yaakov was my life. Prior to *yomim tovim*, instead of taking a vacation, I went collecting, trying to raise funds for a building for Bais Yaakov.

I traveled all over: to London, Paris, Alsace, Florence, Geneva, and to many other Jewish centers. The work was difficult, often with disappointing results, but I knew it was for the benefit of my girls, my Bais Yaakov.

I arrived by boat or train and went to various families recommended by Agudas Yisrael or Dr. Deutschlander. Introductions were made, a car and a chauffeur provided, and then it was up to me.

My first trip was to London, England, where I gave a speech in a very elegant, high-class home. The owners were not religious, but we hoped that they would appreciate the plight of young girls and open their wallets as well as their hearts. The Chief Rabbi, Rabbi Dr. Hertz, came. Standing straight before him, I told him how I originally came from Germany, and now taught in a school in Cracow. I unfolded to him the hardships Bais Yaakov was faced with: the shabbiness of the students' surroundings; the inadequate, cramped quarters; and the dire need of a building. He gave his full support but not everyone gave, and much more was needed.

This was the basic scenario. I would arrive at the city and give a speech to an assembled group of wealthy individuals. To those who could understand the gravity of sustaining an expanding school of girls, I went into details concerning our needs. To others I appealed on a smaller scale, focusing on basic necessities such as blankets, food and clothing. Each place I went to I armed myself with prayers, hope and recommendations.

It was very bitter, hard work. I spent a couple of nights in one place only to travel again to another place. Every night I washed my white blouse, my gloves and collar to look as presentable as I could. Under my arm I carried my papers and letters. Chin up, I stepped down from the platform, my heart beating nervously, my stature impeccably confident. Sometimes I left with tears in my eyes, tears because I did not find support.

Quickly I dashed away those tears, powdered my nose, pulled myself together, and was ready to appeal elsewhere. Some people were helpful, giving money with open hearts and a sympathetic ears, others were less friendly, making my difficult job even harder.

After each trip I returned to Cracow. At the station my students welcomed me as only girls in Poland can, with excitement, warmth and joy at my return. So the years went by, teaching and *shnorring*, and teaching and *shnorring*.

❦   ❦   ❦

After a few years, my parents wanted me to come home, hinting that it was time to think of marriage. I went back to Germany in 1929. There I resumed my studies and completed my university education, receiving my doctorate. This was beneficial to Bais Yaakov for in every education or psychology course I gained more knowledge to give over. My advanced education helped shape the curriculum and methods used in the seminary. Also, my doctorate lent a certain prestige to the Bais Yaakov name.

During that time I became engaged to a promising young student. Isidore Grunfeld was in the process of completing his university education but in Germany one did not get married until after the groom passed his exams and had a profession and a livelihood. He realized how important Bais Yaakov was to me and said, "You go back." And I did.

During the next couple of months I resumed teaching as though I had never left. I taught, *shnorred*, and helped in any way I could in those two months before my marriage. I prepared my trousseau while in Poland. Every article of clothing, linen and even underwear was handmade. I then returned to Germany for my wedding, to begin my life with my husband.

Settling in England

n 1933, when Hitler came to power, the anti-Semitism could be felt in the air. Clients stopped coming to my husband's law firm. It was bad enough to be seen with a Jew by chance, but to willfully seek business with one was intolerable. Jewish businesses, stores, medical and law practices were looted, boycotted or shut down, even during those early years.

The sad question remains: Why did so many friends, relatives and neighbors stay in Germany when such tension was apparent?

Some people could not believe that anything racist and uncivilized would happen in this cultured country of great philosophers such as Schiller and Goethe.

Although I was only a small girl during World War I, I remember how very patriotic we were. My uncles went to war, fighting for Germany. We hoped that the Germans would be victorious. Every Jewish house had a picture of Goethe, and knew his writings. My father was the only skeptic among us. He saw the picture of Goethe and dismissed it, saying: *"Vus zugt a shikereh goy?"* (What does the drunken gentile say?) We stared, aghast: "Papa, how can you say that? Don't you know he is . . ."

It wasn't until World War II that we realized how right he was. Under the cultured, civilized exterior, the Germans were beasts and barbarians.

Still, there were those who remained loyal to Germany. They felt the Nazis were just a leaderless band of ruffians, an unorganized group of hoodlums. People dismissed this reality as a mere threat.

There were also those who refused to believe it would happen. Perhaps if they ignored the situation it would go away. They did not want to leave because they had elderly parents or young children. Some had profitable businesses. For whatever reason, many German Jews remained and, alas, were killed.

Though the feeling in the air was apparent, our decision to leave came about gradually. One day, my husband and I were walking down the street when we heard the sounds of marching behind us. We stood aside to watch the procession. Forward they went, straight and hard as only Nazis could be, chanting their party theme song:

"When Jewish blood drips down the knife, then we'll be doubly strong."

Immobilized we stood, staring at each other. Quietly I said, "Let's go." We knew then that leaving Germany was not a choice, it was a must.

We were a young couple, without small children or elderly parents to worry about. As soon as we got home we began to plan a way to go without attracting suspicion.

Early the next morning my husband walked to the station, carrying only his attache case, looking like any other business man on his way to work. He boarded the train from Wurzburg, where we lived, to the port city of Frankfort.

Four hours later I made preparations to follow my husband. I gave the maid the key to the house and told her we were going to France to celebrate my mother's sixtieth birthday (my parents had moved there several years earlier). I took a small overnight bag, also only equipped with the barest essentials, and walked to the station. A few hours later I joined my husband in Frankfort.

We stayed with friends in Frankfort just long enough to get our papers in order. A few weeks later we arrived at my parents' house in France. We waited there several weeks to see how the situation in Germany would develop. A few weeks later my husband received a letter forwarded to my parents' address.

Dear Sir,

We wish to inform you, that your presence at court is no longer desired . . .

That letter clinched it. We now had to go forward, seek a permanent place to settle.

My husband wanted to move to *Eretz Yisrael* and practice law over there. He went there to case out the situation and see if it was the place for us, while I stayed in France. During those weeks I worked for the refugee office. Aside from being active in refugee affairs, I was busy caring for my baby girl, born a few weeks after our arrival.

Soon after he left, my husband returned to France. Upon arriving in *Eretz Yisrael* the British government informed him that in order to practice law there he must be proficient in the English language as well as British law. And so we decided to go to England for a year in order to learn the language.

❦ ❦ ❦

We arrived in this strange land as refugees, virtually ignorant of their customs and language. For a while, my husband was a "house *rebbi*." There was a rich man, who, for lack of an alternative, sent his children to a non-Jewish school. At the time, day schools were scarce and not yet respected. This man wanted to have someone in his house to teach his children Torah and influence them by being a living example. We lived with that family for several months until friends of ours found us a flat to move into permanently.

During those first years, my husband attended university classes to learn the English language and British law. I began to take in boarders, providing them with a clean room and nourishing food. In addition, I began to teach full time at the Jewish Secondary School founded by Rabbi Dr. Schonfeld.

I was not yet proficient in the English language and it was with trepidation that I entered the classroom that first day. All the curious eyes of the senior boys were turned to the new foreign teacher. I walked to the center of the classroom, stood behind the desk, and made an announcement: "I know I do not speak English very well, but if you pay attention and listen carefully you can learn a lot." This effectively curtailed any plans of making fun of my accent or playing mischief. The air was cleared, they understood I meant business and respectfully obliged.

The first few months were hard. One day I was teaching a geometry lesson dealing with triangles. Usually, the night before class I used a dictionary and made sure I knew all the possible terms that might come up. That day, however, I neglected to do so and I did not know the English terms for any kind of triangle. An idea far. I gave speeches, wrote articles and spread the legend, but I did not go back to Poland.

Then came the first letter asking me to come back. I replied in the negative. I said they should look for someone older, who had learned more and had more to give over. They looked and searched but could not find anyone. After a year, they had not found anyone and were in despair. I decided to discuss it with my parents and we agreed, *bimakom she'ain anashim hishtadel lehiyos ish* (in a place where there are no leaders, strive to be a leader), and so I went.

❧ ❧ ❧

I went to Cracow planning to stay just as long as they needed to find a replacement. Little did I know I would stay there one year, two years, three years and more. Bais Yaakov became the focus of my life. The staff, with the exception of Sarah Schneirer, was very young and inexperienced but this was counterbalanced by the intense devotion and enthusiasm we absorbed from Frau Schneirer.

I encountered many differences between the lives of Polish Jewry and my childhood upbringing. In the material world they were miles apart, with Frankfort a rich community and Poland impoverished. The German Jews were characterized by being reliable, honest and full of energy wrapped in an air of serious dignity. Their apparel was carefully tailored and groomed. In Poland the Jews were less formal, much warmer, their prayers characterized by fervor and intensity. I was attracted to this warmth and friendliness. The girls I met, my pupils, were not as sophisticated as the girls I had grown up with, but their intense desire, their eagerness to learn and friendly open faces endeared them to me.

I must pause to tell of the uniqueness of those first Bais Yaakov students. Never since, have I taught girls so special. I can recall their young voices, so warm and sweet, eager to express themselves. They had complete loyalty to their work and to Sarah Schneirer. They faced the high demands she placed on them in every way they could. She expected absolute obedience from all her students but, in spite of the strict demands made on them, she was loved by all.

I remember one summer afternoon, when all the girls were studying together in the large common room. Frau Schneirer had been away for a week on a fund-raising mission to the provinces. Suddenly we heard a loud clattering of hooves on the pavement ships, even though they were far from home.

In November 1938, Rabbi Dr. Solomon Schonfeld, principal of the Jewish Secondary School, brought a transport of two hundred children from Austria. Accommodations were found for them and they were incorporated into school life. During the months that followed the school grew in size, with many refugee children provided for.

By August of 1939 talk of war began to take on a semblance of reality. I was the headmistress of the Jewish Secondary School in Amherst Park at N16; the pupils consisted of boys and girls between the ages of five and seventeen. We were notified of a government plan to evacuate all schools from London in the event of war. Each school was to be sent to the English countryside for the children's security and safety from possible bombing.

We began preparations for the possible evacuation. Each child was given a rucksack containing the bare essentials for a temporary stay. The rucksacks were labeled with the child's name, school and particular group within the school. Every day the children came to school with their bags, prepared to leave in haste.

The code words were "Pied Piper." Day after day we came to school knowing that perhaps today we would hear the password. With each passing day our group grew bigger as more and more refugee children arrived. Finally, one Thursday morning we received the message: "Pied Piper tomorrow." We told the children that the following day we were having an outing, and they must come to school on time.

Friday morning at six o'clock we were ready. There were four hundred and fifty children, mostly between the ages of eight and fourteen, along with the teachers and fifty voluntary helpers. Line after line, group after group, we left to the station. Two boys led the procession, the *Sifrei Torah* in their arms, proud to be entrusted with such an important task. My own baby was held by his nanny and my two little daughters were under the care of my fourteen-year-old mother's helper.

As soon as we arrived, an officer directed us to board the first available train, just as hundreds of other students were doing. We settled the children down, distributing sweets and snacks, maintaining the calm, unruffled atmosphere of a school outing. The conductor approached me, the "duly accredited teacher of the evacuation party," to whisper discreetly: "This train is destined for

Biggleswade." Now I knew what part of the English countryside we were heading to, but not our final destination.

The trip by train took about an hour. We marched out of the station only to reboard eight large buses, fifty or sixty children to each bus. The ride lasted about forty-five minutes and we finally stopped in a small town's market place.

We were welcomed by many of the residents of the town dressed in their Sunday best. They were rural farm people, good, simple Christians willing to open their homes to evacuees from London. The billeting officer, a tall stately-looking gentleman, stood and allotted each child a place to stay. "I would like four little girls," one lady said. "Can I have two strong boys?" asked a farmer. The groups got smaller and smaller as children were escorted to their new homes.

Suddenly I found myself left alone with the billeting officer. But wait, that couldn't be. There were only four empty buses, yet our school had come in eight! Where were the rest of the children? Where were my little girls and my baby?

"Well," answered the billeting officer, "this is all we have place for here in Shefford. The other children have been sent to the outlying villages of Clifton, Stotfold and Meppershall."

It was then that I began to panic. Where was my baby? Suddenly, as if out of nowhere, a man appeared, pipe between his lips, hands in his pockets. He told us that a man had just come back from Meppershall, and reported that a young foreign girl with a baby had arrived in the bakery there. Immediately I began planning how to get there to claim my child. Noticing my agitation, the man with the pipe offered to drive me there. I accepted thankfully, but I did not breathe freely until I finally held my child in my arms. We went back to Shefford as quickly as possible. It was Friday afternoon, and with all the preparations we had to make for Shabbos, there was no time to lose. At the market square stood Dr. Schonfeld, the principal of the school, who had just arrived from London. He was already making arrangements for the use of the community hall and provisions for a kosher Shabbos meal. After unloading the pots, pans, food and the other essentials that he had brought, Dr. Schonfeld hurried back in his car to make it back to London for Shabbos. Once again I was the sole head of this mission.

First things first. I had to make sure that we were prepared for Shabbos, now just a few hours away. Out on the corner of the main street of town we had our first staff meeting, and already problems were cropping up. Children were welcomed into their foster homes with open arms, friendly faces, and a steaming hot meal — unfortunately, unkosher. Our poor children, shy and tired, shook their heads and took only a few sips of water. Many of these children were refugees from Europe, foreign in dress, behavior and, most important, alien to the English language. The children could not even communicate and tell their foster families why they would not eat. Neighbors began to congregate, speaking about their strange and ungrateful charges.

Several teachers went from house to house explaining the children's behavior. Some were appeased, yet there were still underlying feelings of suspicion and skepticism.

That night we gathered in St. Michael's Hall and had our first Shabbos meal in Shefford. The collation was small, consisting of one sausage, one slice of bread, and many heartfelt *zemiros*. After *davening* and eating, the children went home to their village rooms for their first night in a strange bed.

The villagers were in for another shock, greater than the first. "Johnny, switch the light on so I can see better" . . . "Susie, will you put the kettle on the fire to warm up some water for tea" . . . Each child quietly, shyly, faltering but adamant, replied: "I am sorry sir, but it is my Sabbath today." That night the tired children slept but the town was in an uproar. These foreigners were impossible, it was inconceivable to keep them, they must go.

"Behold the Keeper of Israel neither slumbers nor sleeps" and while we were resting in our beds He was taking care of us. One by one the children melted the hearts of their foster parents with an endearing smile, impeccable manners or winning personality. Less complaints were heard as people began praising their children to each other. Gradually acceptance rather than rejection became the byword.

Slowly they won hearts. The village grocer got in a supply of kosher butter because many women wanted it for their evacuees, so they could have some condiment on their dry bread. The Church Ladies' Guild meeting was postponed because that day was *Lag B'Omer*. Mrs. W. needed to take her evacuee to a good barber in Bedford or else he couldn't cut his hair for another three weeks. Countless such stories are remembered until today. However, this acceptance was far from immediate. It grew as the days went, as we tackled our problems and overcame them. The first step was to see whom we had at Shefford and who was in the outlying townships.

On Sunday, September 3, 1939 all the boys and girls gathered in St. Michael's Hall for roll call. It took all morning to register and identify the children there. Now it was my job to contact the others in Clifton and Meppershall, for they were my responsibility too. I hired an old bicycle for five shillings to ride on to Clifton, a mile away. It was the first time I had been on a bike in fifteen years but, *Baruch Hashem*, I made it. In Clifton, sixty of our children were adjusting to their situation much as we in Shefford were. I addressed my pupils and staff and was prepared to be on my way.

Before leaving I inquired of those nearby. "Has anyone heard any news ..." A young teacher suggested I come to the cottage he was staying at to hear if there was any new information being broadcasted on the radio. I entered the house where a small elderly lady was calmly knitting. "You have just missed the news," she said. I held my breath as I waited for more. "Oh yes," she said, "it's war all right."

My heart sank as my worst fears became reality. Up until now the evacuation had not been a necessity, only a precaution taken with the possibility of returning home soon. Now we knew our stay was indefinite and it could be weeks, months, years before these children would see their families.

The next few weeks were filled with hectic organization. I reunited my family under one roof, established classes and fielded problems. We settled into a daily routine, trying to act as normal as possible under the circumstances. Although we were away from London, out in the English countryside, we heard of the terrible bombings going on over there. We prepared constantly, staging air raids and showing the children how to act in the event of an emergency. Those years were marred by scarcity, blackouts and drills.

Every so often news would reach us that a child's parents had been killed in the terrible bombings. We tried to keep the children happy and patient although some knew they would never see their parents again. Classes went on as usual. *Yom Tov* came and went, celebrated with joy and hope that *"l'shanah habaah B'Yerushalayim,"* next year we would surely be in Jerusalem.

The years passed and finally, in August of 1945, the time came for us to leave. The state of emergency was over and we could all return home. We made a concert performing songs and dances for the Shefford community, showing our appreciation as best as we could. A few days later we gathered on the village square, same buses, same children, only six years older. There were hugs and tearful farewells from many of the foster parents. Some had practically raised their charges, taking them in at six and letting them go at twelve. Few of the ties made there at Shefford were actually severed. For many years letters were exchanged, visits were made, and contact was kept.

The children that boarded the buses in 1945 were different from those that arrived in 1939. They were older not only in years but in experience as well. We had successfully kept a community of children, unified and loyal in *Yiddishkeit*, in a Christian village. Instead of melting into their society, we remained a society of our own, isolated in our beliefs but friendly and accepted as members of their households.

Carrying on

 n 1945, we moved back to London where we resettled the school. During those post-war years, my husband, Dayan Grunfeld, often traveled on behalf of the Chief Rabbi's Religious Emergency Council and actively worked for the British Council for Jewish Relief and Rehabilitation. It was on such business that I accompanied my husband to Cyprus.

During the summer of 1946, the British government began interring illegal Jewish immigrants — en route to Palestine — in Cyprus. They hoped that by detaining these refugees, they would discourage attempts by others to emigrate. However, their attempts were to no avail, and ultimately thousands of Jews were stuck in Cyprus. My husband and I spent *Rosh Hashanah* with these internees.

Davening was held in a tent outdoors. While entering the tent I tripped over a peg and, being British, said pardon to the peg (such is the politeness of the English). As soon as the girls in the tent, whom I had come to befriend, heard this, I was finished. In their minds I was one of the English who were keeping them from entering Palestine. They acted very cold, reluctantly giving me a *Machzor*, not even offering me a seat. My mind searched for a way they would warm up to me.

"Did you ever hear of Sarah Schneirer?" I asked.

"Of course," they replied.

"Well, I was a friend and colleague of hers."

Smiles began to appear on the faces of the girls. They had all heard of the remarkable Sarah Schneirer.

"Did you know Gittel So-and-So?" one asked.

"Certainly," I said. "She was my student."

"I am her sister," the girl exclaimed excitedly, happy to find a link to home.

"What about Rochel So-and-So?" asked another.

"I knew her too," I replied.

"She was my neighbor," remarked a voice in the crowd. The girls had begun to mill around me, eager to hear from someone who actually knew Sarah Schneirer and participated in her legendary work. An amazing thought hit me. The fact that I was married to a prominent *dayan* in London meant nothing to these girls. My university degree and experience as an educator was valueless in their eyes. It was only when they found out that I was associated with Sarah Schneirer that they warmed to me. Although I had left Cracow almost fifteen years earlier, its legacy was with me always.

When my husband and I returned to London I continued to act as headmistress until 1954, when my husband had his first heart attack. I sat in the hospital lounge, waiting for the report of my husband's heart, thinking of the future. I knew that when my husband was discharged he would need all of my attention. Knowing it was the only answer, I wrote my letter of resignation, stating that I was leaving because my husband needed my constant care.

Baruch Hashem, he was given another twenty-one years of life during which he wrote most of his *sefarim*. In 1975 he passed away, and sadly, being that I was no longer needed to nurse him, I resumed lecturing and furthering my involvement in the world of education.

It was through this involvement that I received a most precious gift. I came to New York to speak at a *yom zikaron* (day of remembrance) for Rebbetzin Kaplan. The night before, we had a get-together of all the students and teachers of Bais Yaakov of Cracow now in New York. We asked one of the women to deliver a *d'var Torah*. She thought for a moment and then began to speak.

There is a *medrash* which says that *Mashiach Ben Yosef* was told

Rebbetzin Dr. J. Grunfeld

by *Hakadosh Baruch Hu*: "Wish for anything you like — honor, wisdom, etc. — and I will fulfill it." Answered *Mashiach*: "Give me life."

The question on the *Aggadah* is: What is so extraordinary about this request? He asked for that which any small animal already possesses. Why was his wish for life so special? Couldn't he asked for anything better?

What *Mashiach* was saying was: "I watch the Jews suffer-throughout the generations in *golus*. Let me live in their hearts during these hard times. Let me be their hope. Give me life within their hearts."

As I listened to this beautiful *d'var Torah* I could not believe my ears. It was these very words that I had read from my father's *sefer* to my pupils in Bais Yaakov of Cracow fifty-six years before. Hearing what my father had taught me, and what I had taught them, being retold and taught once again, was the greatest gift anyone could have given me.

flashed through my mind, and quite calmly I drew the shape on the blackboard. Sternly, I asked: "Can anyone tell me what shape this is?" One boy raised his hand and gave the correct answer. "Very good," I said. "Now I want everyone to repeat it three times." By the end of the lesson I knew how to pronounce "isosceles triangle" perfectly.

Another time a boy interrupted a lesson. "Mrs. Grunfeld, Simon is cheating." Now, I had no idea what the word cheating meant, but to show this would be disastrous. I looked at both boys sternly, and said, "I know." This, in effect, rebuked Simon for his "cheating" and the other boy for talking out of turn. Although the problem was solved I still wanted to know what cheating was. When I got home I looked it up in the dictionary, adding yet another word to my growing English vocabulary.

Every morning I had to address the students at a general assembly. Each night I sat up and prepared, checking every word in the dictionary to ensure I was pronouncing it correctly. After a year of teaching I became the school's headmistress. Those years were difficult, with my job at the school, caring for the boarders and raising our children. Then came Shefford.

The War Years in Shefford

(Based on the book *Shefford* by Dr. J. Grunfeld)

t was the summer of 1938. Under the calm serenity and security of daily life were feelings of fear and trepidation. People talked about the political situation: Would there be war? Deep down none of us thought our lives here in England would be disrupted or that the danger was really imminent.

During that year, many refugee families emigrated from Eastern Europe. Organizations were set up to help people get visas, passports and transportation.

Sometimes families were unable to leave and parents sent their children to safety. Many organizations were set up to transfer groups of children, some as young as five years old, who had been pulled away from the security of a home and thrust into a foreign world. They were reestablished, attended schools, formed friend-

Rebbetzin Basya Scheinberg

> " The strong influence and the chinuch
> we received from home more than
> compensated for our meager formal Jewish
> education and relatively small circle
> of religious friends. We knew that
> our family was different, special. "

Rebbetzin Basya Herman Scheinberg was born and raised in New York's Lower East Side. She married Rabbi Chaim Pinchus Scheinberg and in 1930 the newlyweds traveled to Mir, Poland, joining a few other American families living and learning there.

They returned to New York in 1935, where her husband devoted himself to learning and *chinuch*. In 1960 Rabbi Scheinberg founded Yeshiva Torah Ohr; five years later the Scheinbergs, together with the *yeshivah*, moved to *Eretz Yisrael*, where they reside today.

Yiddishkeit in America

e lived on the East Side of Manhattan, then the center of Torah Jewry in New York. Although New York, in the early 1900's, was very different from today for *frum* Jews, there were several large *shuls* and *yeshivos*.

We *davened* at Tiferes Yerushalayim, a *shul* established in 1925. The five story building was beautiful and elaborate, with a *bais medrash*, women's section and several classrooms. My brother went to *yeshivah* there from the time that he was four years old, leaving in about fifth grade, because the school did not go higher. For high school he went to Rabbeinu Yaakov Yosef, the *yeshivah* established by my maternal grandfather.

A new *yeshivah* had been founded by R' Yehuda Hershel Levenberg, Chief Rabbi of New Haven, Connecticut. This *yeshivah* was patterned after the European *yeshivos*, with no secular studies. It was the first and only of its kind in America at that time. This was the type of *yeshivah* my father sent his son and students to. From there he recommended that they go on to European *yeshivos* for more intense study.

Although the community was growing, there were no *frum* schools for girls to attend. When we reached school age, about six-years-old, my sisters and I were sent to public school. After our classes we attended the National Hebrew School on East Broadway. All the girls from observant homes went to Talmud Torahs such as this one. Our teachers were mostly women who taught us to read and write Hebrew. My father never really approved of this school and when he discovered some of the teachers were not strictly *shomer Shabbos* he withdrew us.

From the time we were very young, my father engaged a tutor to come to the house daily. He taught us the basics of reading and writing Yiddish. We had always known how to speak Yiddish because, although we children always spoke English, my mother would speak to us in Yiddish. He taught us how to read, write and understand basic Hebrew, though not through *Tanach* or any *seforim*.

My father wanted us to go beyond the little we had learned in

Hebrew school, and beyond the basic language understanding we got from our tutor. Each week we read over the *parshas hashavua*. We were supposed to try and learn the *Chumash* on our own time by reading a *Tanach* with English translation. As an incentive, Papa rewarded us with a prize after every *parashah* we finished.

When we were little we had only that Hebrew-English *Chumash* from which to learn. Every week we read the *Tz'ena U'rena* on the *sedrah*, which gave us a better insight into the lessons of the *Chumash*.

Because we had such limited opportunities to learn, my father instilled in us lessons of *hashkafah* (values), *mussar* (Torah ethics), and philosophy through his endless stories of *tzaddikim* and *gedolim*. He was our library of English stories about great *Yidden*.

❦ ❦ ❦

I was thirteen-years-old when I graduated junior high school. The standard age of graduation was fourteen; however, I had taken rapid-advancement classes and therefore met all the requirements for graduation a year early.

When my older sister Esther had completed junior high, my parents were faced with a dilemma. My father felt a girl that age could not continue to go to public high school for, although the public-school system was exceptionally well run, boys and girls had classes in the same building. This was not a good atmosphere for future *Yiddishe* mothers. Therefore, Papa began his search for the best alternative. That was when he discovered the Hebrew Technical School for Girls.

The name was misleading, for they taught absolutely no Hebrew subjects. It was a private, secular, girls' high school run by Jewish, non-observant people. We were too old for Talmud Torah, and so our formal Jewish education ended. The school was exemplary in every other way. Instead of a standard four-year high-school program it had a two-year program without summer vacations. The school had a healthy and enjoyable athletic program which my father felt was beneficial for growing girls.

We also had a choice of classes to choose from. I took the commercial program so I could learn practical office skills such as bookkeeping and typing, skills that would help me find a job after I completed high school.

The friends I made in school were mostly "school friends" whom I generally only saw in class. Many of my classmates were not very *frum* and so my father preferred to keep those friendships to a minimum; I was never allowed to go to them for long visits or for Shabbos. We could not socialize on the phone because, although we owned a telephone, most other families did not. I was very close with the few religious girls that came to visit me at home on Shabbos. We did not really have any places to get together and have "fun."

It was unheard of for young *frum* girls to spend the day shopping all over town by themselves. Besides, there was so much to do at home, we never really had that much time to spare. There were no official Bnos groups on Shabbos afternoon but because it was the only day to get together, it became the main time when friends came to visit.

The strong influence and the *chinuch* we received from home, more than compensated for our meager formal Jewish education and relatively small circle of religious friends. We knew that our family was different, special. We could not do everything the other girls did. Even in the hot summer months of New York we had to wear uncomfortable tights and long sleeves. My father insisted that these laws of *tznius* (modesty), were the trademark of a Jewish mother and should be kept with pride. We learned to ignore the pitying looks of friends and neighbors and wore our "uniform" all through the year.

We also had more chores and work to do than our friends did. Our days were monopolized by preparations for guests, especially on *erev* Shabbos. People came to the house at all hours of the day and night knowing they would get a hot nourishing meal and a bed to sleep in. My sisters and I always had to be ready to help by *shlepping* cots, making beds, changing linen or washing dishes. After one shipment of *orchim* (guests) would leave we had to help clean the house and prepare for anyone else who might appear at the door.

It was always a special treat to have *gedolim* (great men) as our guests. Great men such as Rav Shimon Shkop and Reb Moshe Mordechai Epstein stayed in our house. They slept in our home and often ate with us, while they were in America collecting for their *yeshivos* in Europe. Rav Baruch Ber Lebowitz and Rav Eliezer Yehudah Finkel both stayed with us for a year and a half on fund-raising "business." We learned a lot from them, not only in matters of Torah and wisdom, but in modes of behavior as well. They were always so appreciative of everything we tried to do to make them comfortable. They had left behind large families of their own, and often spoke to us small children about them. One impression that remains in my mind is how they always had time for us. Whether it was just a smile or a short conversation they made us feel important, not like insignificant children. They left my family with beautiful blessings that I am sure have helped us through the years.

❦ ❦ ❦

I learned a lot from the way my mother ran our home. It was she who cooked the tremendous amounts of food needed for our many guests. She always saw to it that every guest had a clean bed and a hot nourishing meal. Her modesty and piety were apparent in her every action and we learned from her example, trying to live up to her model.

I remember a particular man who came when I was a small child. He appeared at the door one day in need of a place to stay. He was suffering from an infected foot. At that time there was no penicillin, and any household remedy people recommended was tried. Someone suggested that he light some straw, hold it near the wound and let the heat permeate the skin to draw out the infection. This cure was very hot and painful. It was hard for him to administer it to himself so someone came every day to help him. The infection itself was very painful and prevented him from having anything touch his foot. He sat all day with his bad foot propped up in a chair. If he ever had to go somewhere just around the house he always had to *shlep* the chair with him. He stayed in our house for several months until he was well enough to go out on his own. My mother always stressed the importance of making these unfortunate people feel happy and comfortable during their stay, regardless of the inconvenience.

Although we, *Baruch Hashem*, had no financial problems because my father's business adequately supported us, many others were not so lucky. Every Thursday night my mother took me with her to bring food to families who could not afford to buy much for themselves. There were no welfare programs and, during the hard years of World War I, and later the Depression, many people did not even have enough to eat. Mamma and I went to bring some of these families staples, such as flour and sugar, for Shabbos.

Once in a while my mother found time to go to visit her relatives but usually they had to come visit her if they wanted to keep in touch. She rarely went out just in case there might be someone in need of a place to stay or a meal to eat. Her days revolved around preparations for *orchim*, the family, or *yomim tovim*. My only outings were occasional trips to the circus or the park. Sylvia, my best friend, was an only child and at times her mother took us places.

❧ ❧ ❧

Shabbos and *yom tov* were busy times for us at home. We always had extra guests to cook and clean for. It was also a time to forget everything secular. On Shabbos my father spoke only Hebrew, for there is a special *kedushah* to *lashon kodesh*.

From *Rosh Chodesh Elul* through the *Yomim Noraim* the atmosphere in our house was one of something extraordinary approaching. Papa prepared us by talking about the importance of *teshuvah* (repentance) at the table daily.

Finally, Yom Kippur arrived. The entire family went to Tiferes Yerushalayim. My father was the *baal Shacharis* there for forty years and Mr. Listoken was the *baal Mussaf*. As children, we could not stay in *shul* all day without getting restless and rowdy. My father's sister lived nearby and part of the day would be spent there with my older sister supervising. As we got older we stayed in *shul* where we *davened* as much as we could, and then we went out to play.

As teenagers, we were old enough to join our mother but even then we sat all the day in the back on a bench. It was only proper for us to give the married women the better seats.

Immediately after Yom Kippur we started building our *succcah*.

For most of my childhood years we lived in a house without an available roof or backyard. We used to build *our succah* at a neighbor's. This family had a store whose roof we used as our *succah*'s foundation. We had to go through the neighbor's kitchen to get to it, but this was not too inconvenient since they ate with us anyway.

Our *succah* was large enough to accommodate our family, theirs and our many guests. We children spent hours decorating our temporary dining room to be cheerfully comfortable for *yom tov*. Before *yom tov* my father went to Canal Street on the all-important mission of finding the most beautiful *esrog*.

One of the best parts of *yom tov* was having my father home for an entire week. He never worked during *Chol Hamoed* regardless of the lost income. We usually used this time to visit relatives, grandparents, aunts, uncles and cousins.

Simchas Torah was not only the end of Succos, it was the highlight. We all went to Tiferes Yerushalayim to watch the men dance. My father rejoiced so, that he used to jump up almost to the ceiling as he danced.

Each *yom tov* had its own preparations characteristic of it; Pesach more than any other. There were no products kosher for Pesach or *shemurah matzah* (*matzah* made of flour watched since it was harvested). My father went to Goodman Bros. factory and obtained permission to personally supervise the first batches of *matzah*. He even began taking orders from friends and neighbors or relatives who also wanted these special *matzos*. Papa also wanted to make *charoses* available for anyone who wanted. We helped him prepare large amounts of *charoses* to distribute to anyone who asked. We filled up small white cones and handed them out as needed.

After a while my father added more products to his list of Pesach foods by hiring *mashgichim* to oversee the processing and packaging of items such as prunes and spices. Nevertheless there was plenty that we did not have. *Chalav Yisrael* (dairy) products that were kosher for Pesach as well were unobtainable, including plain milk. In fact we didn't even have *milchig* dishes or silverware for Pesach. When there were babies at home, my mother had one saucepan set aside to warm up milk.

In all the preparations we children were never overlooked. It was very important that we each got a new dress or outfit in honor of the *yom tov*. We looked forward to wearing our special clothes and eating the special *yom tov* food. Even Pesach time when there was so much else to do, Mama remembered the sweets we craved. She ground a lot of carrots and mixed them with sugar and ginger to make homemade candy.

Yom tov in America, when I grew up, was very different from today in that it was not commercialized at all. Each holiday was a private family affair that non-Jews hardly knew of. Jews were less public about their celebrations. Purim, for example, was a wonderful *yom tov* where everyone was lively and excited. However there were no elaborate costumes in the streets or people publicly dressed up. My mother spent most of her day in the kitchen preparing food for our tremendous Purim *seudah*, and lots of *shalach manos*. The only break she had, was to pause and listen to my father read the *Megillah* in the house. My father was also busy, gathering all the *shalach manos* together to personally deliver them to friends and neighbors.

At the meal, some men got a little high and lightheaded but no more than that. Yet their simple joy was pure, *"yom tov-dik"*, and beautiful.

Chanukah was celebrated in very much the same way, purely and simply. We had no special or elaborate *menorah*. My father took a large piece of wood, upon which he set up eight little *schnapps* glasses. He filled each with olive oil and carefully lit them in front of the window. It was such an unusual sight. Out on the streets the atmosphere was full of preparations for the non-Jewish holiday. Home was a haven to take in the holiness and peace of our simple *menorah*.

Moving On

 finished high school when I was sixteen years old. In those years most observant girls went to college, to train to become public-school teachers. A teacher did not have to work on Shabbos and most *yomim tovim*, something required in more glamorous jobs. Even menial workers had a six-day work week. The only other position open to single girls, that did not require college, was secretarial. However, it was hard to get a job as a secretary in a Jewish office that kept Shabbos. My father would not allow me to attend college classes but *Baruch Hashem* I found work in a Jewish office. I was there for about two months and then I started working in my father's real estate business. This job did not last long either, for my "career" would soon end with my marriage.

The average age when American girls married was generally over twenty. My father, however, insisted that his daughters marry young. This way there would be a rapid transition from the shelter and security of her parents' home to the shelter and security of her own home and husband. Such a situation would leave little time for exposure to outside influences. Once a girl is on her own too long she becomes independent, with ideas hard to regulate. Of all my sisters I was married the youngest, at seventeen.

My parents made me a beautiful *chassunah* in Hennington Hall. There were no special kosher halls, so my father went to the hall and *kashered* all the pots and silverware. He not only made sure that the catering was done by the most trustworthy firm but also personally supervised the slaughtering of the chickens.

I do regret we did not have a professional photographer there. We had a table of thirty of the greatest *gedolim* in America at the time. We went to the studio to have a wedding picture taken and that's the only one we have.

❦ ❦ ❦

It was April of 1930 when my husband and I boarded the boat bound for Europe. We were embarking on a journey as foreigners to a strange land for, although my husband was born in Poland, he had left as a child and had no recollection of his birthplace. With trepidation, and the usual fear of the unknown, we were on our way.

For six days we traveled by ship. The weather was beautiful, but nevertheless seasickness overtook me and I was ill most of the time. We stopped at Liverpool, England and then at France, where we disembarked. From there we took a passenger train departing for Poland. Two days later we reached Warsaw, and, exhausted, tumbled out of the train right into the customs officials who were to examine our possessions before allowing us to pass over the border into Warsaw.

When we had arranged our trip we knew that we would have to stay in Warsaw for Shabbos. The *mashgiach* of Mir, R' Yeruchem Levovitz, had recommended a family for us to stay with and we made arrangements before we left.

By the time we arrived it was almost Shabbos and we had to leave the port as soon as possible. The officers assured us that they would guard our belongings over the weekend and no one else would get near them. This was true — no one else got near our luggage, because those very guards made sure that only they could steal our goods. When we returned many of our possessions were gone. What a welcome!

We finally arrived in Mir on May 1, 1930. We got a big *baruch haba* (welcome) from my brother Davie and his wife. They had been the first American couple to come to settle in Mir after their marriage, and set a precedent several others followed.

We tried to get settled as soon as possible so my husband could comfortably begin the post-Pesach *z'man* (semester). My brother and sister-in-law arranged for our apartment and furniture to be ready as soon as possible. By the start of the *z'man* we were pretty well entrenched in Mir.

My husband's schedule was basically routine. He went to learn as usual, coming home for meals. I, on the other hand, had to face momentous changes. It was very lonesome to be far away from family and friends, in a place so different from home.

Our first apartment was not really an apartment at all, it was one large room in a rather small house. My landlady and her family lived in the smaller rooms of the house, and we shared a kitchen.

In the summer we used a special side room as a summer kitchen, so that the stove would not heat the whole apartment.

In the beginning of our stay this arrangement was more than satisfactory. I did not know how to cook very well and my *balabuste* (landlady) had to teach me everything. Lesson number one was how to use the stove.

I was used to modern New York where we had normal gas stoves and ovens. Here I was confronted by a large monstrosity that they told me I was supposed to be able to cook in. This *kachal* stove, as it was called, extended from floor to ceiling, allowing the smoke to leave through the chimney. Large quantities of wood were used to fuel it. Every morning at six o'clock the Polish woodchoppers rode into the *shtetl*, their wagons piled with the logs of wood they had cut from the forest. They bartered their goods until ten o'clock. My *balabuste* took care of purchasing and storing the wood so there would always be some available. Every morning someone had to collect enough chopped wood for the day and bring it inside. Several pieces were put into the front of the stove. The burning wood became live coals that provided heat, for comfort and cooking. The comfort part was easy but the cooking part was quite difficult. There was a special long stick on which you had to attach the pot of food. It required a certain knack to get the food in, without any mishaps and cook it for just the right amount of time.

My initial shock when I came to Mir was at its backwardness. I had never been in a place where there was actually no running water. Even in Warsaw, where we had stayed that first Shabbos, there had been modern plumbing. In Mir, the watercarrier came every morning, a pail slung over each shoulder, attached to a wooden bar that lay across his neck. He walked from the nearest well to the house and came inside. Careful not to spill a drop, he poured the two pails into one large pail in the kitchen. That was the entire water supply for the day. After using the water to wash dirty dishes or clothing, we dumped the water outside, for there were no drains. The bathrooms were all outhouses and there were no baths to speak of. *Baruch Hashem* I was young and able to adjust quite well. However, I was lonesome and at times homesick. During the first year, I cried more often than I was happy.

My *balabuste* was an elderly woman who lived with her daughter and grandchildren. While her daughter cared for the children, she tended to the cooking and upkeep of the house. We stayed with them for about a year, after which we moved across the street.

Our new apartment was larger and more comfortable than its predecessor. Although we still had to share the kitchen, we now had a living room and a bedroom, a one hundred percent enlargement. The new home brought several changes — I finally learned how to bake, an essential talent since the bakeries sold very little: maybe some *challah* and sponge cake. An added advantage was that my new *balabuste* owned a cow, which meant I now received milk, cheese, butter and other dairy products.

Being one of the first and only American families in Mir, we often invited the American *bachurim* for Shabbos. They, like us, were a long way from home and we appreciated each other's company. Other than that we did not do much visiting. Winter began in November and did not end until well into April. For almost six months you could not leave your house because of the freezing weather. The temperature was often twenty-nine degrees below zero and one could not go anywhere unless bundled up very well. The native residents of Mir were more accustomed to the climate then we Americans, and consequently they dealt with the freezing weather better than us. Aside from the men who had to go to *yeshivah*, we barely ventured outside. We stored most of our food supply inside.

Our cellar was quite cold and a perfect storage place for the potatoes, onions and carrots. We also stored apples but they only lasted until Chanukah time. From Chanukah until spring we had no fresh fruit at all. However, throughout the winter we had the jams and preserves that we had canned during the summer time.

Bananas were unheard of; in fact I do not think that the people of Mir had ever seen one! As for vegetables, cucumbers were available only in the summertime, while tomatoes or green peppers were non-existent.

Once, I went to the market and saw a cart selling corn. I was excited to find another vegetable that was both delicious and available. The Polish peasant selling the corn was surprised that I wanted to buy it. *Kokorooys*, as they called it, was used as animal feed and it was known that most *yeshivah* wives did not raise animals. I took home my prize and asked my *balabuste* to show me how to plant it. When she heard I planned to eat the corn she looked absolutely shocked, but nevertheless she showed me how to plant it.

We planted the corn in the spring. That summer we went to a small town in the mountains called Laviellna. It was a beautiful place where many of the *yeshivah bachurim* and families went. The climate was mild and pleasant, a wonderful break from the harsh winter.

When we returned to Mir I eagerly checked on my corn. The vegetables were full grown and I immediately cooked some.

Delicious! My *balabuste* and neighbors thought we were crazy and were sure we would be poisoned. There was one woman whom we had hired to make *lukshen* (noodles), a talent I had not yet mastered. (Ready-made *lukshen* could not be bought.) She saw me eating the corn and told me how she used to eat it when she had lived in Russia. I was more than happy to give her a piece and she enjoyed it immensely. After several years, others saw that we were far from being poisoned and they too began to eat our corn.

Before we left, people began planting tomato seeds on their window sills but when I was there we did not have any. My *balabuste* worked hard planting the few common vegetables we had, such as cucumbers, potatoes and onions. We used to pickle some of the cucumbers during the summer but these did not last through the winter. We lacked all these fruits most of the year, and we missed them a lot.

In our first year there from the end of June through July, we went on vacation to Luna, Poland, which is near Gradno. We stayed in a small hotel in a nice area in the country. My sister-in-law, Chaya Dube, had her first child in the hospital in Slonim. They planned to hold the *pidyon haben* there just before the *z'man* was scheduled to start. We decided to arrange our itinerary to include a visit to the Chafetz Chaim. When my father had journeyed to Poland several years before, this had been the highlight of his trip. We, too, did not want to pass up such an opportunity. From Luna, we planned to travel to Radin, from there to Slonim, and then back to Mir.

We went by train to a city near Radin and from there we took a mini-bus to the famed town. The trip itself was memorable. I bought a bottle of seltzer in case I should feel ill along the way. Seltzer used to come in glass bottles with a cork cap to keep the air out and the bubbles in. On the way, without any provocation from me, the cork popped off the bottle and flew to the front of the bus. The seltzer *shpritzed* all over the place, soaking me and my fellow passengers. It was very embarrassing and I was extremely relieved to finally reach our destination.

We arrived at the house of the Chafetz Chaim, and were ushered into the front room. The house was nice but sparsely furnished with only the bare essentials — a table, chairs and a bookcase of *seforim*. As we sat and waited for an audience with the *gadol hador* the Rebbetzin served us tea and jam, the customary offering to the guests. I was a bit nervous and only drank a little of the tea. Nevertheless, nausea overcame me and I felt I was going to be sick. I ran to the window just in time but was terribly embarrassed. The Rebbetzin was kindness itself; smiling at me knowingly, she told me not to worry for it was a healthy illness I had.

We were ushered into the Chafetz Chaim's room. It was practically bare, with only a few chairs for visitors, a table, and a bench with a pillow on which the Chafetz Chaim sat. He was learning quietly, with only his large *Gemara* before him. He was ninety-five years old at the time but his large smooth forehead and shiny face belied his age. The young boy who showed us in introduced us, informing him that we came from America to learn in Mir. His eyes lit up as he responded warmly, "If *Hashem* could come down to give the Jews the Torah, then a couple can come from America to learn in Mir." He then gave us a nice blessing for fine *Yiddishe* children. We then asked for a *brachah* for a couple who after several years of marriage had no children. With a sad look in his eyes he sighed and said that they should live long lives. This cryptic answer was puzzling but today we can see its meaning. Apparently this couple was not meant to be parents but the Chafetz Chaim's blessing came true, and they lived happily for many years. After our short conversation we left him learning, for he never wasted a precious moment.

Two years later, while we still lived in Poland the Chafetz Chaim was *niftar*. All over the globe the Jewish people mourned its great loss, but nowhere was the feeling as intense as in Poland. Some of the *bachurim* of the *yeshivah* wanted to attend the *levayah* (funeral) very badly. They set out together but were stopped by a guard who would not let them proceed. In order to travel from city to city within Europe one had to carry an I.D. card stating information vital to the government. The *bachurim* were from several different places and some did not have all the necessary certificates. Using this excuse the guard refused to allow the entire group to go any further. Disappointed, they turned back home. The next day we learned that that very same guard had died. We clearly saw how *Hashem* pays back evildoers for their wickedness.

After the *levayah* we met someone who did make it there. He did not have enough words to describe the tremendous crowds of people that attended, the moving eulogies delivered and the loss each and everyone felt.

We decided to go to R' Chaim Ozer Grodzenski for a *brachah* because several weeks after our visit to the Chafetz Chaim, I was having some difficulties with my pregnancy. While we were there, his Rebbetzin advised me to seek a well-known doctor in a larger city; *Baruch Hashem* he was able to help.

I gave birth to my first child in Slonim, a city nearby. There were no hospitals in Mir, and I heard that there were more advanced medical facilities in Slonim. We traveled by sleigh as far as the train station, where we boarded a train to Slonim. The city was much bigger than Mir, full of stores and people, with about fifty *frum* families. We stayed there about a month. For Shabbos we went either to an aunt and uncle of my sister-in-law or to the home of the Slonimer Rav.

Although our stay in Slonim was pleasant, I was disappointed with the care I received at the "modern" hospital. The atmosphere was depressing, the accommodations were bad, and the nursing care insufficient. I never bothered traveling to that hospital again. The next time I needed such care I stayed in Mir and used a midwife.

We had lived in Mir a total of five years, arriving after Pesach of 1930 and returning in 1935. My husband had been born in Poland, and had moved to America when he was nine years old. Therefore, my husband had dual citizenship, Polish and American. The law stated that he could not stay in Poland for over two years, or he would lose his American citizenship. After the first two years were over, we applied for a two-year extension enabling us to stay a total of four years. By then, we were already seriously planning to go back to America. I had even made arrangements to sell some of the belongings we did not want to bring along. Then my husband went to talk to R' Yeruchem, the *mashgiach*. He urged my husband to stay because he was learning well and progressing so far. My husband agreed, and we decided to stay. I had been so sure that we were leaving; now I was heartbroken with disappointment. It had been so long since I had seen my parents and I was really looking forward to going home. As it turned out, we did not stay much longer but went back later in March.

America — Eretz Yisrael

 hen we got off the boat in America we had exactly eight cents with us. That eight cents could not go far, specifically, not as far as my parents' house. Therefore, we told my parents when we were coming, so they could pick us up.

Before we arrived, my parents rented for us an apartment very close to them. Its location and cheap rent were the good news. The bad news was that it was unpainted, dilapidated, and in altogether bad condition. We lived there for six weeks, until after my third daughter was born.

We were able to move because my husband got a job as the *menahel ruchani* (principal) and *mashgiach* in Yeshivas Chafetz Chaim. At least he now earned a salary, fifteen dollars a week. He had been offered several jobs outside New York City for up to a hundred dollars a week, but my husband turned them all down. He was only interested in a position with active involvement in a *yeshivah*. My husband was very young, almost the same age as the graduating class. He was their *mashgiach* even though he could have been their classmate. Until today they have sustained relationships of more than *rebbi* to *talmid* but as friends as well.

Once a man appeared at our door selling *seforim*. He had a second-hand *Gemara* in good condition which he wanted to sell for a considerable amount of money, and we really could not afford it. Every time someone came to the door selling a *sefer*, my husband would buy it, and I knew that this time would be no different. I asked the man not to tempt him with the *Gemara* because although he would want it, we really did not have the money. The salesman answered me, "If your husband was training to be a surgeon and someone came by selling small, sharp knives and tools, would you stop him from buying them?" When I heard these words, I realized their importance. These *sefarim* were the "tools" my husband needed for his profession, the tools of every *ben Torah* and *talmid chacham*.

Although there had been some religious progress in America since my childhood, one thing had not changed. My oldest daughter went to public school until she was twelve years old because there was no Bais Yaakov. However, not much later Rebbetzin Kaplan opened the first Bais Yaakov in America and my daughter was one of the first to register. The rest of my girls went to Bais Yaakov in Williamsburg for most of their school years. My son attended R.J.J. for elementary school and then we sent him to Telshe Yeshiva in Cleveland, Ohio, until graduation.

❦ ❦ ❦

In 1960 my husband opened his own *yeshivah* called "Torah Ohr." For several years the *yeshivah* grew. One day my sister Ruchoma came back from her trip to *Eretz Yisrael* very excited. She had just decided to buy the first apartment to be built in a new settlement called Kiryat Mattesdorf. I had been in *Eretz Yisrael* several times to visit my father but never before had we seriously considered moving there. My husband and I discussed her purchase and decided that we also wanted to move to *Eretz Yisrael*. So, with most of our savings, we too bought an apartment there. In 1965 we moved to *Eretz Yisrael*.

We were one of the first families to settle in Kiryat Mattesdorf. We arrived with about six other families, among them our own son and daughter and my sister Rebbetzin Esther Stern. We brought the *yeshivah* along — some twenty-two young *bachurim*. When we arrived, the *yeshivah* building was not yet built, so we rented the top floor of the Diskin Orphan Home. Little did we realize that there we would stay for five years until our own building was ready.

In 1966, we were able to lay the cornerstone of the *yeshivah* building. Then came the 1967 war and all construction came to an abrupt halt.

There were plenty of warnings of the war's imminence. In fact, many people left *Eretz Yisrael* out of fear, but my husband refused to do so. However, we realized the gravity of the situation, and gave the *bachurim* of our yeshivah the option of going home. Several of our boys left but they were sorry that they did, for the war lasted a total of six days.

During the war we practically lived in the bomb shelter for our own safety. We had no kitchen in the shelter and I had to go upstairs to cook our food. Once, I went to cook a chicken that I had in the freezer when suddenly a bomb hit nearby. Trying not to panic, I grabbed the pot of chicken and ran all the way back to the shelter, the sound of falling bombs echoing in the air. Breathlessly relieved, I reached safety. Those few days, when people were dying and we were isolated, ignorant of the situation, we lived in fear. *Baruch Hashem*, it was over soon and was a great triumph for *Yiddishkeit*.

When we were finally able to walk around *Eretz Yisrael*, we saw there was a lot of damage done both in *Yerushalayim* and in Mattesdorf. We were finally able to go to see *Har Hazeisim* where I could visit my mother's *kever* (grave), and the *Kosel Hamaaravi* (Western Wall). In 1972 the *yeshivah* building was completed and we moved in.

Part Two

Sarah Schneirer

he working day is over, and Sarah Schneirer, the expert dressmaker, steps outside to leave. The bitter Polish wind whips her face as she turns homeward. In the distance she can see her brother returning home from his day in *yeshivah*, together with a friend. They are discussing some kind of problem they encountered in their learning. Her brother's face is animated and his friend is gesticulating wildly. As they enter the house behind her, her father picks up on the topic and joins in.

The discussion is now getting even livelier and more heated, as each argues his point. Sarah Schneirer leaves the living room, for the discussion is beyond her comprehension — obviously the men's domain.

She enters the kitchen and sees her mother poring over the pages of her beloved *Tz'enah Ur'enah*. Her sister avidly reads the pages of a Polish novel.

To the daughter of a fine family of Polish *chassidim* living in Cracow, this scene seems in no way unusual. As the eldest in the family, when times grew hard she felt responsible to contribute. She taught herself a trade, and soon earned a reputation as an efficient dressmaker. Day in and day out she would measure, trace, cut and sew, turning out beautiful outfits for her customers.

As her nimble fingers flew, her equally agile mind turned to her customers. They would spend so much time surveying themselves critically in the mirror, she mused, anxious that their dresses be perfect. But while they were occupied with their beautifully clad bodies, they were neglecting their *neshamos* (souls). Dressed in the height of fashion, they were spiritually clad in paupers' rags.

And the dressmaker, Sarah Schneirer, dreamed a dream. How she wished she could teach them, make them see where their real happiness lay!

She found few who shared her concerns. The older generation seemed to have withdrawn into a spiritual world of its own, unaware of the potential for tragedy among the children. Teenage girls, educated in Polish gymnasiums, yearned for modernity. Their mothers found fulfillment in prayer and simple faith; their brothers in the challenging world of *yeshivah* and Torah study. And the girls? They were left with the feeling that Jewish life was a burden and the Torah itself outmoded.

The busy dressmaker saw disaster facing Jewish women, but lacking a formal education, lacking experience in teaching and public speaking, she saw no way that she could help stem the tide of assimilation.

Growing Up

arah Schneirer, like most Jewish girls in her homeland, attended Polish schools, completing eight years of elementary school with honor. It was during those years that she was nicknamed "The *Chassidonis*" (the righteous girl). Already her piety and interest in religion was becoming apparent.

She loved to read, and when absorbed in a book could be totally oblivious to her surroundings. But her greatest joy came from the *sefarim* that she treasured: a *Chumash* with the *Chok Le'Yisrael* commentary brought to her by her brother, and the *Tz'enah Ur'enah*, the timeless Yiddish classic. On Shabbos afternoons, when other girls would gather for a few hours of singing, gossip and good times, young Sarah would sit in a world of her own, lost in her *sefarim*.

But the quiet, studious youngster saw more than just the pages of print before her. She often visited a neighboring woman whose oldest child had run away from the home she found too confining, marrying without *chupah* and *kiddushin*. Sarah would gaze at the woman's youngest child, the only one whose eyes still lit up when Shabbos came, and wondered how to preserve that glow of joy.

She watched the trains grow full each Elul, with thousands of *chassidim* traveling to spend the holidays with their *rebbe*. Fathers and sons waited eagerly the year through to make the journey and spend *yom tov* in the atmosphere of holiness. And the women? They stayed at home. The mothers pulled unwilling daughters with them to *shul*. There, the older generation poured out its heart to the *Ribbono Shel Olam*, tears streaking their cheeks. The young girls stared with a mixture of fascination and contempt, yearning to be outside, far away.

When their fathers returned home from the *rebbe's tisch* they were too excited, too blinded by the *kedushah* they had experienced to see the grim reality before them. While they had been dancing to the rhythm of the *Yomim Noraim*, their daughters had been dancing in the opposite direction. Their paths had grown further and further apart.

The busy seamstress saw this, with all the clarity of her unusual, sharp mind. She saw and dreamed of setting these girls back onto the paths of their fathers.

The Development of a Teacher

er dream might have remained nothing more than that, idle thoughts to enliven the workday of sewing, but Providence intervened.

The Great War broke out.

In 1913, Sarah Schneirer and her family fled war-torn Poland, and found refuge in Vienna. Still "The *Chassidonis*," her first thoughts were for the upcoming Shabbos Chanukah: She must find a *shul* where she could *daven*. Following the directions of an obliging landlady, she entered the *shul* of Rabbi Fleisch of the Stumperfergasse.

What followed was a revelation. The *rav* addressed the congregation, spoke of Maccabees, their challenge and their heroism. He spoke also of Yehudis and of what a Jewish woman could accomplish. Something stirred within Sarah Schneirer's heart as she listened, enthralled, to his gripping words. If only she could magnify his voice and deliver his words to all the Jewish women and children that she so longed to reach. How could they ignore their appeal?

She became his most avid student, never missing a sermon or *shiur*, doggedly writing down each lesson. Her efforts to gain knowledge for herself, in order to eventually give it over to others, bore fruit, with the assistance of a kindly Providence whose intervention was sometimes startling. One evening, despite her best efforts, the thread she was using to sew with kept breaking. Finally, seeing that she was accomplishing nothing with the stubborn thread, she left early and made her way to the *shul* to hear Rabbi Fleisch speak — arriving just in time to hear him, as he had, without announcement, begun earlier than usual.

Nebulous dreams of teaching Jewish women were beginning to take shape, were growing clearer in her mind. Someday she would pass these inspiring words of Rabbi Fleisch on to other women, who so needed to hear them. To ensure that her small part in transmitting the *mesorah* (tradition) of the Jewish people would be perfect, she overcame her shyness and showed Rabbi Fleisch himself her notes. The *rav* was impressed with their accuracy and with the almost photographic memory of this unassuming seamstress. He suggested that she study the works of Rabbi Shamshon Rafael Hirsch and Rabbi Marcus Lehmann; by eating only one meal a day she managed to save enough money to buy one of Hirsch's *sefarim*.

With war's end, Sarah Schneirer was ready to return to Cracow — and ready to give over all that she had learned. All she had to do was find someone to listen.

It wasn't easy. Her efforts to reach out to women and older girls met with little success: To them her words sounded strange and outmoded. And then she turned to the children, beginning with only five. They listened, they learned, they remembered her lessons, so simple and effective were they:

"How do you get bread?"

"You buy it in a store."

"With what do you buy it?"

"With money."

"But where does the store get the bread from?"

"The baker delivers it."

"With what does the baker bake bread?"

"With flour."

"From where does he get the flour?"

"From the mill."

"What do they grind in the mill?"

"Wheat from the farm."

"How does the farmer get the wheat?"

"He plants the seeds, fertilizes, waters and cuts the grain."

"How does it grow? With the sun and with rain? And who gives us the rain and sun? *Hashem*. And how can we repay Him? With gold and silver? He doesn't need our money. We can repay Him with a *brachah*."

The school grew. After one year, more than eighty students were crowding to hear the classes, all given proudly in Yiddish. A larger apartment was rented. Former students, barely out of class themselves, were pressed into service, to teach those still younger.

The school grew; a movement was born. In 1924 a quiet, motherly woman attended the convention of Agudath Israel, the organization that was such a strong force in the life of Polish Jewry. Her fierce determination and her beliefs communicated themselves to the assemblage, and Agudath Israel began its involvement with Bais Yaakov, enabling the movement to grow in a way that even Sarah Schneirer would not have dared envision. Shunning personal aggrandizement, Sarah Schneirer willingly welcomed the contributions of more experienced educators, allowing others to build on her own accomplishments.

The Seminary

In a small side street in the Cracow ghetto, in a large tenement fronted by narrow stone steps leading to crowded flats, stood the Bais Yaakov Seminary.

It was not much to look at, but it was a beginning. There was a small kitchen with a curtain separating it from the main room: A bright, sunny area, alive with the sound of study during the day, was transformed into a bed-lined dormitory at night. Here the young girls would take their places, sitting on chairs or on crates, intent to do their work.

Frau Schneirer's first class consisted of twenty-five girls, none older than sixteen. They studied hand-written texts penned by their teacher, learning a methodology that was at the same time simple and effective, pages and pages of lessons designed to keep bright, eager children interested and excited about their Jewish heritage.

Even as she trained the teachers to teach, she helped establish the schools for them to teach in. She traveled the length and breadth of her land, accompanying her young charges as they embarked on their new adventure of teaching in — and often founding — Bais Yaakov schools. She spoke to groups that were sometimes interested, sometimes hostile, urging the opening of still another school.

The quiet seamstress stood at the head of a vibrant, growing movement — and yet she remained the same Sarah Schneirer of old. In Elul of 1931, at the ground-breaking ceremony of the new seminary building in Cracow, as she watched her dream come to fruition, Frau Schneirer, ever the model of *tzinius* that she taught her students, took her place with the crowd, leaving the limelight to others who had built upon the foundation that she had laid. Flanked by her beloved students, she whispered a silent *tefillah*, thanking

---

Sara Schneirer's Ethical Will

Dearly beloved daughters,

What can I possibly say? Man envisions and plans many things, but the will of *Hashem* predominates.

Now at this hour of parting, I truly feel the ties so closely connecting me to you, my daughters. I am sure that the force of my feeling is reciprocated. I hope and pray that the tears you will shed upon reading this, will reach the Throne of Glory, where they will have a profound effect on the future of *klal Yisrael*.

My daughters, I feel it necessary to warn of two things which may hinder you in your efforts to attain fear of *Hashem*. Firstly, beware of pride — avoid a feeling of haughtiness that can persuade a person to think that he is worthy of praise and honor. Secondly, avoid the other extreme, a feeling of low self-esteem and hopelessness.

Daughters, you have successfully completed your formal schooling. The hardest test of all awaits you — life. Life may provide you with many trials and tribulations, but you are well armed. You fortification is fearing, loving, and serving *Hashem*.

Your sainted teacher and mentor, Reb Yehuda Leib Orlean, said after administering the seminary test, "You have successfully proven that you have acquired the knowledge to both learn and teach. The question is whether you will be able to implement it and enlighten young Jewish souls."

Strengthen yourselves, my daughters. Never tire of devoting yourselves to the sacred work of *Hashem*.

I wish to share the following *pesukim* with you, that will accompany and guide you through life.

עבדו את ה' בשמחה   שויתי ה' לנגדי תמיד
למנות ימינו כן הודע   ראשית חכמה יראת ה'
תורת ה' תמימה משיבת נפש

May *Hashem* guide you and watch over you, my children. May He listen to your *tefillos* and redeem His people. Amen.

Yours,
Sarah Schneirer

G-d for having brought the movement so far in such a short time, and praying that prosperity should not bring on complacency.

She was young, only fifty two-years old, when she was *niftar*, after a difficult illness. Even on her deathbed, she was still teaching, still writing, still penning lessons for her students:

> And now, my dear daughters, you are standing before the severest test, that of life itself. For some life is hard but in your hands, by the blessing of the L-rd, are strong weapons of defense. They are fear of G-d, reverence, love and service of Hashem.

She died looking at the Shabbos candles she had kindled moments before, a pure soul whose nimble fingers had woven a glorious garment for the Jewish girl.

Eim B'Yisrael

by Rebbetzin Chana (Gulewsky) Gorfinkel

aruch Hashem, I have had a lot of *mazal* in my life, but what I consider myself most fortunate is in being one of the first students of Sarah Schneirer. I was *zocheh* (meritous) to sleep in the same building as her with only one wall separating my room from hers. I saw her day and night, her everyday actions. She was a piece of perfection in her devotion and love to *Hashem*, *b'nei Yisrael*, and the pure souls of *Yiddishe kinderlach*, Jewish children.

The year I went to Bais Yaakov Seminary in Cracow was 1929, a terrible year. The winter was the coldest in many decades. Even the old generation could not remember such a harsh winter. The trains could not run because the tracks were frozen. In cities large and small there were food shortages because many fields had frozen over, ruining valuable crops. There were also difficulties in transporting available produce from farms to cities.

Through all the towns, hamlets and large cities of Poland there were long breadlines. We had to stand in the bitter cold and snow to get bread. Compounding the cold and famine was the depression. Rich people, who had owned property and businesses and were accustomed to a life of luxury, found themselves penniless. They could not pay their mortgages or bills and many committed suicide.

It was at this time that I was supposed to journey from Mir to Cracow. It was extremely difficult to find anyone willing to make the twelve-kilometer journey by sled to the station and consequently my parents had to pay double the standard price. I arrived in Cracow to find the cold was just as bitter there as in Mir. People were unable to heat their homes so the government set up iron ovens in the main streets for them to warm themselves.

That winter I became sick for the first time in my life. I had a very high fever that kept me from sleeping. As I lay awake in bed, light from a keyhole caught my eye. I glanced at my watch and saw that

---

* Rebbetzin Chana (Gulewsky) Gorfinkel was one of the early Bais Yaakov Seminary students. After she finished her schooling there she taught in a *shtetl* in Poland. She married R' Chaim Garfinkle who later taught in Yeshiva of Brooklyn.

it was four a.m. I was amazed that someone was up at that hour. Although I knew it was not a nice thing to do, curiosity got the best of me. I got up and peered through the keyhole. In the midst of oceans of paper sat Sarah Schneirer. Her hand held a pencil on which she rested her forehead, eyes closed. I stood still, my feet glued to the floor. I could not understand why she was not in bed at this hour. After about ten minutes she lifted her head and glanced at her watch. "*Oy vey*," she exclaimed, "I slept ten minutes and I have so much to do!"

I returned to bed but was unable to sleep as I was so impressed with what I had seen. Her table overflowed with letters, papers and books, and she just sat and wrote without stop. There were no published teaching manuals or books and she had to fill notebooks by hand with her lessons. She was sending information and teaching plans to alumni of the seminary with positions in schools of their own.

A half hour later I saw Sarah Schneirer walk into the bedroom. What will she do now? I puzzled. She walked from bed to bed, untangling jumbles of bedclothes and picking up fallen blankets. Lovingly, she covered each girl as a mother does for her child.

It was by seeing her devotion in preparing lessons to be taught to *bnos Yisrael*, daughters of Israel, and her protective attention of the girls under her care, that showed me how she had earned the title of *Eim B'Yisrael*, Mother in Israel. She had so much love for her students that it could only be compared to that of a mother.

Not one of us ever wanted to do wrong or disappoint her in any way. The hurt in her eyes was the most effective discipline. We knew she actually hurt inside when one of us acted badly and we loved her too much to intentionally hurt her. It warmed our hearts when we saw her appreciate something we did well. Her eyes, her face, her whole being would grow alight with the joy of our accomplishments. She tried to teach us love and patience by example. We saw how she never raised her voice or lost her temper and we desperately wanted to emulate her. She taught without giving lectures of punishment, but with love, devotion and praise.

The apartment we lived in was one of many in a tenement. Our accommodations were cramped because Sarah Schneirer wanted to have as many students as possible regardless of the lack of funds. There were no separate classrooms and bedrooms. During the day we would sit on crates and chairs to learn our lessons while at night we cleared the room and unfolded the beds to sleep on. One very cold night, it took many hours for us to fall asleep. As a result, the next morning we overslept. In order to start classes on time we hurriedly put away our beds with less care than usual. One girl accidentally pushed a bed into the door, breaking the expensive glass. We were afraid of Sarah Schneirer's disappointment in us, that she might be angry at our carelessness. Nervously we all stood, silently staring at the glass shattered on the floor. Sarah Schneirer broke the silence and asked, "Is anyone hurt?" At our negative reply she sighed and said "Baruch Hashem." Without another word she calmly proceeded to sweep away the fragments of glass. Her concern was not for the expensive glass but only for the welfare of her girls. She gave us no mussar but her concern made us determined to be all she expected of us. In every minute of her life she was completely under control. Her good-heartedness was apparent in every deed. How lucky we were to have had such a teacher from whom we gained not only "book" knowledge but knowledge of how to live.

When we went home in Nissan and Tishrei to spend yom tov with our families, she wrote to us. She was like a mother who never forgot her children and we were like children, eager to hear from home. I had many letters from her, each one a masterpiece full of practical wisdom and Torah thoughts with deep lessons to understand.

Bais Yaakov was a unique institution. It was not only a place to learn Tanach, Tehillim, Yahadus, etc., but a place to perfect one's midos. Everything taught was supposed to become a part of us, not just a sentence in a notebook.

Sarah Schneirer emphasized several themes over and over. "Shivisi Hashem l'negdi tamid" — Hashem is constantly with you. You must serve him with happiness, as it says "Ivdu es Hashem b'simchah." You must fulfill all mitzvos bain adam l'chavairo, the command-ments having to do with relationships between people. "Kabed es avicha v'es emecha," honor your father and mother, and "Hevai mekabel es kal ha'adam b'seiver panim yafos," greet every person with a friendly face. These phrases were part of our everyday lessons, conversations and, more important, actions.

Before lessons we said the tefillah of Avinu Av Harachaman. We begged Hashem to have mercy and give us sechel to understand and glean knowledge from one thing to another. We must learn, and we must also teach. We must fulfill the mitzvos with love for Hashem. We must rejoice in being bnos Yisrael and having the Torah. We must try to be near Hashem and feel that He is with us and is always watching. This is how we prepared ourselves for learning every day.

The Life of a Bais Yaakov Girl

by Rebbetzin Basya (Epstein) Bender

he Bais Yaakov in Cracow was legendary in Poland. It was the dream of hundreds of bright *frum* girls to be able to learn there. I, too, dreamed of attending the famous institution.

We arrived midday, one hundred and fifty-seven excited, nervous girls full of life, hope and anticipation. We came from all over the world (although mostly from Poland), virtual strangers but kin in spirit. For we had a common creed, a common goal: to learn and absorb all we possibly could, to be able to become teachers who would spread *Yiddishkeit*.

I had traveled ten hours by train from Otwock to Cracow. It was an expensive and long trip, but many of my classmates had undergone longer and more expensive journeys. The *mesiras nefesh* our parents had in sending us away was tremendous. They were sending their young girls on a journey from which they would not return for almost an entire year. And yet they were proud to say their daughters went to Bais Yaakov in Cracow. We not only wanted to succeed for our own sake, but for the pride of our parents as well.

The first person I saw was Sarah Schneirer. Her smile and welcome washed away any homesickness I might have felt.

We felt we were in the presence of a strong personality. Her bright intelligence and her warmth won girls over immediately. We were able to see her *ehrlichkeit*, her *shlaimus* (perfection), her purity just from that first meeting. A sense of belonging, us to her and she to us, developed. She made us feel that we were at home.

The first three months were a trial period. Through our studies, social interaction and class performance, we were judged as to our

---

* Rebbetzin Basya (Epstein) Bender attended Bais Yaakov in the 1930's. She later married R' Dovid Bender, a *menahel* in Yeshiva Torah Vodaath. From the time they arrived in America until today, she has been teaching in Bais Yaakov Seminary.

teaching capabilities. Bais Yaakov did not have the facilities or teachers to educate all girls that wanted to attend. The demand for new teachers was tremendous and every day the *hanhalah* (administration) received pleas for more teachers. Therefore, they could not merely educate girls; they needed to train them to be teachers. If, after three months of watching and observing the girls, our teachers felt there were those that were not capable of teaching, they were to be sent home. We had to sign a paper stating that we agreed to these conditions before starting school.

Everyone knew they had to do their best and most diligent work in order to stay. Nevertheless, approximately two thirds of the girls in my grade were told to leave. This was a tragic time for these girls. Their hopes and dreams had been shattered and they would now have to return home without having accomplished the goal for which they and their parents had strived. Shortly after my year in seminary, more teachers became available and this system was stopped. It was too painful for the students.

Our days were filled with interesting and stimulating classes. Though each group had almost every teacher for one period or another, there was one main teacher in charge of each class. My homeroom teacher was Fraulein Doctor Rosenbaum. Of all the teachers in the school she had the most influence over me. In general, she was a popular teacher and many girls in other classes were jealous that my class had her so often. She taught us *Chumash*, *Navi*, *Hashkafah*, and a Torah perspective of psychology.

"Fraulein Doctor," as she was called, was a rare combination of a solid *Yiddishe* outlook and knowledge of the world as well. Her strong yet practical character made her more than a teacher — she was a friend, a confidante we could all relate to, someone who could talk to and understand girls from varied backgrounds.

After her marriage to Dayan Grunfeld and subsequent move to England, she earned the title of "The Queen": We already saw these qualities emerging. Her aristocratic bearing had no taint of snobbery or pride. It was simply a part of her — something one noticed just by being in her presence.

Sarah Schneirer was our teacher as well as our principal. However, aside from what we learned in her classes — the wonderful lessons on *Pirkei Avos*, *Tefillah*, and *Hashkafah* — we learned much more just from being in her presence. Even in a casual conversation one of her unique *vertlach* always surfaced. Not only

„Beth-Jakób" Sommer-heim 1930

were they insightful pieces of *divrei Torah*, they were spiced with her special sense of humor and sharp wit.

She was a role model we learned from just by observing. Sarah Schneirer had a nice fur coat, a luxury most people would appreciate, yet she never wore it in Cracow. We all wondered why this was so: If she had this coat, why not wear it? One day she explained her reasons to us. This coat was special to her but not because it was expensive or because she wanted to look nice. It was special because when she went to collect *tzedakah* dressed in the impressive fur coat, people respected her more and donated more money. We could hear the amazement in her voice — "people actually made judgments based on appearance?!?!" Incidents like this were numerous.

Dorm life was fun filled and left no time for homesickness. Eating, sleeping and learning together for months on end created strong and lasting friendships among many of us. After classes we were free to do what we wanted. The dormitory echoed with the sounds of girls studying, completing assignments or just talking. We were allowed to go off school grounds as long as we received permission. The school was not unusually restrictive; they had a responsibility for each of us and had to make sure they knew of our whereabouts. There is no reason for girls to just go anywhere at anytime at will. We understood that we had to be responsible and account for our movements.

Officially, there was no such thing as vacation. Summer as well as winter was spent in intense study. We were permitted to go home to our families for Succos and Pesach, but only for the length of the *yom tov*. Going home for Rosh Hashanah and Yom Kippur was optional for they did have a special program for these *yomim tovim*.

In the middle of *Chodesh Elul* the school picked up and went to the mountains. It was a beautiful area with open spaces, fresh air and blossoming trees. The peaceful atmosphere was conducive to learning and meditation. The program was designed for teachers, students and alumni. We had *Hashkafah* courses, given by Rabbi Orlean and other teachers, appropriate for the approaching *Yomim Noraim*. Day after day we prepared to truly be able to face *Hakadosh Baruch Hu* on the Day of Judgment. The culmination of all our work came on Yom Kippur, and *motzaei* Yom Kippur the dam broke. We were so caught up in the day's holiness and intensity that after the fast, instead of running to eat, we began to sing and dance. Where we found strength I cannot imagine, but we just kept on dancing. I can remember clearly how our voices rang out to the tunes of *ashrei ha'ish* and *v'taher libeinu* and how we danced in circles around and around and around. We then heard *Havdalah* and broke our fasts. To me, this was the nicest time in school — and the one that made the biggest impression on me.

In the summer the seminary would rent out a farm in the country. We brought up the dishes and cookware from the city and prepared to spend the summer in an educational but relaxing manner. Classes were held outside under the trees, to absorb the fresh air. We took advantage of the beautiful world *Hakadosh Baruch Hu* created, and we learned in this pleasant atmosphere.

❧ ❧ ❧

The Mercaz was an organization that regulated the educational system of Bais Yaakov schools. They would send the seminary in Cracow a letter saying what type of teacher they needed for what type of school. Based on the amount of children in the classes and the family backgrounds of these children, the seminary would choose a girl. Some girls were better at teaching a large number of students, while others were good only for older children, and teachers were sent accordingly.

After graduation, girls were not allowed to go home. Under the Mercaz system, directly after completion of their studies in Bais Yaakov, girls were sent to their teaching positions. Teachers were in great demand and time was precious. Letting girls go home would be a waste of that precious time.

Girls were never sent to teach in their hometown. The Mercaz felt that among family and friends girls would be distracted from the job they were trained for and their attention would turn to *shidduchim* and home life rather than their students. At this time the establishment of Bais Yaakov was crucial and preceded all else.

My class and I graduated Chanukah time rather than at the end of the year because of the demand for teachers. It was wintertime in Poland and I had to travel alone on a train to the city of Radamsko where I would embark on my career. The seminary had grown considerably and there was not a large-enough staff to have anyone accompany new teachers to their jobs. Every turn of the train's wheels led me further away from the safe security of my beloved Bais Yaakov and closer to a city of strangers.

When I arrived at the station I was to hold a specific Yiddish newspaper which was supposed to identify me as the town's new teacher. Sure enough, several women approached me to confirm that I was the incoming teacher. They took me to a small apartment that was to be my home as long as I stayed. The town provided me with room and board.

The children I taught went to public school for their secular subjects and in the afternoon they came to my class for Hebrew and Yiddish *limudim*. It was a challenge to appeal to the children of many different age groups at one time. I was there for only six months and in June I was transferred.

The school in Otwock was much more advanced. It had a nice building with more children, a larger staff, spacious classrooms and adequate school supplies. In this school they had secular studies in the morning and *limudei kodesh* in the afternoon. The *hanhalah* of the school needed a new teacher, and had approached the Mercaz to request that I be sent to teach there. They knew my parents, family and my capabilities as a teacher and therefore specifically asked for me. The Mercaz did not want to violate their rule of not sending girls home and if I taught in Otwock I would live at home. For some reason, an exception was made and I was sent. I was very excited to finally be able to live at home after two years of being away from my family.

Wherever I lived, I knew I would teach if I could. Bais Yaakov instilled in us the will to give every Jewish girl a Bais Yaakov education.

Her Legacy Lives On

*by Rebbetzin Grunfeld**

hen I first met Sarah Schneirer, she was forty-two years old. I saw a motherly looking person clad in a plain black dress. Her lively face was framed by black hair done in an old-fashioned style. My first impression was a woman full of liveliness, simplicity and motherliness, not the pioneering personality of a movement.

It was midsummer when we met in Robov, an isolated retreat in the Carpathian Mountains. She came, with a group of thirty girls around her, to meet my coach. Actually, it couldn't have been called a coach for it was more like a horse-drawn cart. Only such carts traveled from the railroad station to such remote, tiny villages that didn't even appear on most maps. There I was, a weary traveler who had just traveled past gypsy cottages and caravans to reach this tiny little hamlet.

My curiosity mounted as I watched her approach. I had heard that Sarah Schneirer was a remarkable woman. It was said that she worked as a dressmaker by day, but studied tirelessly at night until she had enough knowledge to teach others. Then, she shared her own room and food with a group of young girls while training them to be teachers. I knew that she already succeeded in gathering to her about fifty girls. They lived with her and shared her meager meals all in order to absorb from her as much knowledge as they could.

The simply dressed, motherlike figure walked along with a swarm of girls around her. They were all lively and talkative as they bustled around her. My cart parked by the roadside and they all swarmed around it. I already began to feel at home when I heard the friendly words of welcome they called to me. I was lifted out of the rickety cart and Sarah Schneirer embraced me in welcome. Some of the girls tended to my luggage and paid the driver while others swept me down the road. I found myself seated on a wooden bench

---

* See Rebbetzin Grunfeld's interview in Part I for background.

under a tree in front of a small cottage. The "Mother" sat next to me and began to unfold her dreams and the beginning of its accomplishment. From that moment on I was under her spell.

This mother of Yisrael was a unique personality. She was blessed with a sense of humor and liked to hear stories, jokes and riddles. In the beauty of nature she saw an illustration of *Tehillim*. Psychology and science found their meaning for her because they could be used in the service of *Hashem*. Even the new fur coat we persuaded her to purchase she bought only because it had a special purpose: It would enhance her prestige, which in turn would lend importance to Bais Yaakov in the eyes of hostile outsiders. She had no *yetzer hara* — neither for honor nor for money nor for any worldly possessions. Her only desire was directed toward the fulfillment of *mitzvos*. She always started the Shabbos meal by exclaiming in a joyful, almost chuckling voice, *Likavod Shabbos Kodesh* (in honor of the Shabbos). After this she would partake of the delicious food.

She was always busy, always active and always lively. Time was a present from *Hashem* and she spent every moment of it in *mitzvos* and in building Bais Yaakov. Yet everything she did was with a peaceful cheerfulness that was intrinsically part of her personality.

I would not describe Sarah Schneirer as a person with "intellectual thirst." Her main characteristic was an unshakable *emunah* (faith) within her. She needed no intellectual proofs, but was delighted when she found beauty and illumination for what she had already accepted. Her mind was not a "searching mind" that looked for answers and proofs. It was a delighted mind, delighted in sharing the truth of Torah with everyone who came in touch with her.

Her pupils did not cling to her because of her knowledge or her speeches. It was the spark of her magnetic *neshamah* that captivated all who came in contact with her. As a magnet attracts iron, this *neshamah* of Sarah Schneirer attracted all other *neshamos*, by her *hislahavus* (zeal) and burning *yiras shamayim*.

She was different from anyone I had ever met. She was whole hearted, without any conflicts in her personality. I am not a mystical person, but I really think she was born with perfect *temimus* (completeness) and as such had the healing power to mend the breach in Jewish homes, where the sons attended *yeshivos* while the daughters were kept ignorant and left the path of Torah and *mitzvos*. Sarah Schneirer was a model of *tzinius* in every area. At that time, all wigs were made of human hair for there were no synthetic fibers. Sarah Schneirer did not feel that these wigs adequately met the requirements of *tznius* because they looked too much like real hair. She found a wig made out of "peller", a type of material that looked something like hair but was not nearly as attractive. This was still not enough and she covered this wig with a scarf on Shabbos in *shul*. She had no vanity for her personal looks because, she said, beauty in the eyes of *Hakadosh Baruch Hu* is *tzinius*.

Although many of the students had cameras and loved to take pictures, she refused to be photographed. The only photo of her that exists is the passport picture she had to have taken before she went to Vienna. Like most passport pictures, it is not true to its nature. There is, however, an impression done of her by one of her pupils that is fairly accurate. One year, in honor of her *yahrzeit*, some of the present Bais Yaakov leaders wanted to distribute copies of this impression. I could not allow this, for she was against such picture-taking in her life and therefore it wasn't right to go against her wishes after her death.

❦ ❦ ❦

Sarah Schneirer was only fifty-two years old when she succumbed to a short but fatal illness. She was still in the midst of the work she pioneered in the establishment of Bais Yaakov. She died as she lived, kindling lights. It was an hour before Shabbos and she asked for the Shabbos candlesticks to be brought to her bedside. Then she lit the candles for the last time. They were still burning when her soul had returned to its maker.

Her students, who had been *davening* for her recovery, were heartbroken. Thousands had known her personally and felt an irrevocable loss. They all knew that the rest of their days they would feel her eyes upon them and her presence among them. Her dreams still had to be fulfilled and they were her emissaries. The only way they could face her again in Eternity would be to live life the way she would expect them to. This was the impact of Sarah Schneirer on all she came in touch with.

We have to thank her for the women she raised, women who are happy when their sons learn well and who are determined to marry only *bnei Torah*. After the near-total devastation of Torah life these women helped reconstruct *Bnei Yisrael.*

I believe *Hakadosh Baruch Hu* sent Sarah Schneirer for her short term of fifty-two years to accomplish all she did. The *Kaddish* of heartbroken pupils was their declaration that they were determined to carry on what she began.

As Sarah Schneirer becomes a legendary historical figure, people are inclined to forget her valiant assistants. Many of these young teachers — so sweet, wholehearted and generous with their devotion to their students — were taken away from us very young. We must not forget these devoted girls who were essential to the Bais Yaakov movement.

Her most outstanding pupil was Channah Grossfield Biegun, affectionately known as "Hanka." She came to Bais Yaakov at the age of fifteen, full of life and worldly inclinations, the exact opposite of Sarah Schneirer. Sarah Schneirer had no desire for anything other than Torah life while Hanka was already attracted by the various secular lures. She worked very hard to become the student Sarah Schneirer expected. After passing through all the stages of self-discipline demanded by Sarah Schneirer, she was able to go from the type of life that had taken her away from parental guidance and become Sarah Schneirer's first assistant in the seminary. After Sarah Schneirer's death it was Channah to whom Bais Yaakov students looked as the foremost woman teacher.

One cannot forget Lacia Sharanska Wasciat. In those difficult years when Bais Yaakov had to squeeze itself into the tenement flat of the poor Cracow ghetto, she saw to the health and well-being of every girl. During the first few days of school, the students were so intent on their studies they paid no attention to their everyday needs. It was she who went about, in her own quiet way, setting up kitchens, healthy dormitories and sickbeds. Everyone was made comfortable and felt at home because of her care.

Esther Hamburger, Esther Goldstoff, Gittel Teitelbaum, Bela Gross, Chaya Rosenbloom, Ida Bauminger and Esther Heitner were some of the young, vibrant and brilliant teachers of the Bais Yaakov. They were trained in the movement and went on to become lecturers in the seminary. Without them to keep the movement alive, it couldn't have blossomed as it did.

There was Yehuda Leib Orlean, Alexander Zische Friedman, Gershon Friedenson, Senator Moshe Deutcher, Reb Ascher Spira, Freilich and Meir Heitner. We have to record and remember their

*Fraulein Esther Hamburger,
of the first teachers
in Bais Yaakov.
She was educated in
Germany and came to
Poland as a young girl.
She later married
and continued her work
in chinuch all her life.*

names here because they have no graves or tombstones. They contributed so much to the success of Bais Yaakov. There are many other names of people who helped Bais Yaakov with all their hearts. The continuation of the Bais Yaakov movement, and the building of Torah homes by Bais Yaakov-trained girls, is their *Kaddish*.

Although all these beloved workers and the students perished in World War II, Bais Yaakov survived. The Bais Yaakov spirit gave strength to thousands in their last hours. We can see a glimpse of this from the farewell letter written to the world by the "Ninety-Three Bais Yaakov Girls." These students of Sarah Schneirer gave their lives *al Kiddush Hashem*. Those that survived Bergen-Belsen, Auschwitz and World War II carried the Bais Yaakov tradition wherever they settled. That is why throughout the four corners of the world Bais Yaakov lives on.

An American In Cracow

by Rebbetzin Chava Weinberg Pincus

ver since I could remember I had begged to learn like my big brother. My father would playfully say, "Just get a boy's suit, tuck your curls under a hat, and go to the *yeshivah*." When I was a very little girl I didn't respond to this, but inside I thought, "Why not?" It wasn't until years had passed that I really had my chance.

I was a twelve-year-old child, when my father came home one day in great excitement over a report concerning the founding of a Bais Yaakov School in Poland. He had received a copy of the "Agudah Periodical" from Poland which contained a report about a fabulous woman, Sarah Schneirer, a real *yarei shamayim*, who had started a school for girls in Cracow. At that time there were, of course, no day schools in New York where religious girls could receive a *frum* education, so we were obliged to attend public school. There were Talmud Torahs with afternoon classes a few times a week for boys and girls, but my father, being the *mechanech* (educator) that he was, would not let me attend these classes because they were not conducted by *bnei Torah*.

My father was sure that the Cracow School was the solution for the proper school for his daughter and he was ready, right then and there, to ship me off to Sarah Schneirer. However, my mother — understandably — was not happy about this. To send a child so young, to a land so far away, to a place so utterly strange was just too frightening, to say the least.

In 1932, when I graduated high school, my father again brought up this "far-fetched" project. Mother at the time was in *Eretz Yisrael* with my younger siblings. She had been ill and the doctor had recommended a warmer climate. But instead of going to Florida, as he advised, she went to *Eretz Yisrael*. My father and I were

---

* Rebbetzin Chava Weinberg Pincus, the author of this chapter, went from America to Cracow in 1932. She later married Rabbi Chaim Avram Pincus, a *rav* in New Jersey and later in Williamsburg. She has dedicated her life to the furtherance of *chinuch*.

resolved that I would go to Cracow for a year's study with Sarah Schneirer.

When word got around about this plan, our community of observant, committed Jews buzzed with the exciting prospect of my going and many could not believe that we were really serious. For a young girl to travel to Europe in those days, and of all places, to Cracow, was odd indeed and quite incredible!

In retrospect, I imagine I was quite adventurous and daring ... but in truth I must have been rather scared and uncertain of what I would find there. I wanted to go but I made a condition that I would have a round-trip ticket and be allowed to return whenever I would want ... (just in case!)

My knowledge of Poland was very sketchy. From the stories of the Baal Shem Tov and *tzaddikim*, I gathered that it was a vast land with many forests and many *goyim* who hated Jews, and where Yeshiva *bachurim* "*essen teg*" and "*trinken treren*." Evidently, despite all the care to shield me from the Haskalah, some of it did get through to me.

The day of departure arrived. Our Bnos and Zeirei Agudas Yisrael had been very excited for weeks about my trip. I was given a "story book" send-off. My cabin was crowded with friends and well-wishers. Bnos girls from Brooklyn, Manhattan and the Bronx came — with flowers, knickknacks and a lot of stationery for letter writing — to bid me a "bon voyage." The excitement and anticipation was overwhelming and "Bais Yaakov" was on the lips of all.

My trip was a far cry from today's average thirteen-hour "hop" by airplane. I sailed the ocean "blue" for six days. A family from Slonim was traveling on the same ship and Father, no doubt, counted on my staying close to them. We met in the kosher dining room of the ship where we managed by eating salads, sardines and hard-boiled eggs.

The ship docked at Bremen, Germany, from where we started on a long, tedious train ride over a substantial part of Europe. It was on this part of the trip that I first witnessed a hatred for the Jew and the anti-Semitism of the Poles. I did not know then that there were first, second and third-class compartments on European trains. My travel agent had arranged for my ticket to take me from New York to Cracow, which included a third-class train ride from Bremen. The train was very crowded, the benches were hard, and the cabins not very clean; apparently, someone had thrown up in our car. The conductor, who came through to check our tickets, got a good whiff of the rank odor and saw the filthy mess. He looked around, took hold of an innocent *chassidishe* Jew and began to shake him and scream at him. I, a young, spirited, liberal American, was shocked. I stood up and in English — which at that time was still respected a little — called out to the conductor: "What makes you think he did it? I've been here all the time and know he is innocent, so please take your hands off and leave him alone." Taken aback, he let the Jew go. That upsetting incident engendered a hatred in me for the Polish people, their language and everything connected with them. Nor was it the last experience I had with the Polish anti-Semites.

❦ ❦ ❦

At long last I arrived in Cracow. I had expected to find — if not a "red carpet" rolled out — at least some sort of delegation to give me a warm welcome and provide the necessary transportation to get me to my long-awaited destination. Needless to say, I was bitterly disappointed. I found myself standing alone, left forlorn in the middle of nowhere, with no one to turn to for help. (Subsequently I learned that through some misunderstanding, Rabbi Jung's office in New York had notified Dr. Deutschlander in Vienna of my coming, instead of contacting the *hanhalah* in Cracow.)

I approached the driver of a *drushka*, a horse and buggy. I showed him the address of the Bais Yaakov Seminary — Stanislavska ten. He shrugged his shoulders. No such address. I tried to convince him, using every language I knew, that it was the right address — or very similar to it — but to no avail. I looked around for a Jewish face, also in vain. Finally I had an inspiration. I signaled to the driver to put my valises on his *drushka*, and motioned to go! I figured that we were bound to find ourselves on a street on which I would see a Jew who would surely be able to direct me to the seminary. That is exactly what happened. I saw two *chassidishe* men, stopped the *drushka* and inquired of them the address of Bais Yaakov. I thanked them and noticed how mystified they were by my appearance and strange Yiddish accent and, most of all, by my destination, Bais Yaakov — of all places! Soon after, much of Poland would hear about the "Amerikanke" who came all the way from New York to study with Sarah Schneirer in Bais Yaakov. The address, by the way, was Stanislawa ten!

My problems and difficulties were not yet over. It was the middle of July when I arrived. I found the building almost deserted. Sarah

Schneirer was away working for the establishment of a new Bais Yaakov school. Fraulein Doctor (as we called Reb. Dr. Grunfeld) was away on a mission representing Bais Yaakov in some other country (I think it was Italy, and the family she tried to interest in Bais Yaakov was called Pachifichi). The seminary consisted of two courses of two classes each (about one hundred and twenty girls) who were away with their teachers on a three-day outing. No reception. No welcome sign. No one to greet me except Vikchu, the Polish servant, and a few girls who, for some reason, could not go on the trip. Someone went to fetch Mrs. Kasirer, the cook and housekeeper.

By this time I was just ready to burst into tears. I was tired, hungry, homesick and terribly disappointed with what I saw. I went up to the first landing where I could look out of the window and shed my tears without being seen — or so I thought. I found out later that I fooled no one.

I kept asking myself: What did I do? Why? Where have I come to? Just looking at my surroundings depressed me even more. Actually I found myself in a new modern building with large airy classrooms upstairs and a beautiful dormitory with showers and baths. The downstairs, however, — which was meanwhile the only part I saw — had not yet been completed. It was not yet plastered or painted and did not enhance my first impression of Bais Yaakov. Even the few girls who greeted me could not lift my spirits. They were so different and spoke in such a strange Yiddish, I just couldn't relate to them at all.

I remembered my round-trip ticket and the "deal" I had made with my father. I kept feeling my bag to make sure the ticket was still there. Yes, it was right there ready to be used. I was already making plans to return to New York right after Shabbos.

In the meantime Mrs. Kasirer, the housekeeper-cook, appeared, arranged to put my valises in the dispensary room on the first floor, and sent up a tray with food for my lunch. It consisted of a slice of bread with a half-fried egg and half-fried onions. I mention this because I was a spoiled, finicky eater and could not get myself to eat a half-fried egg, especially with half-fried onions! But my hunger won out and I decided to try just a small piece of bread. I dipped it into the egg and onions. Very soon the bread, egg and the onions were gone, and I had finished my first meal in Cracow. After this — finicky me — learned to eat whatever food was served as long as it was kosher and clean. To be completely honest I must admit that it took me quite a while to get used to — for example — the "little slice of sweet fish" on Shabbos *kodesh* instead of the peppery fish we had at home. But eventually I made peace with that too.

❦ ❦ ❦

The following afternoon all the teachers and students returned and the school was back in full swing. I got to know some of the teachers who were to become not only my very good teachers but also very close friends. Some of the Lithuanian girls who befriended me then — and who were not so long after destined to reach our shores — became my lifelong, dearest and most precious friends.

Then started the preparations for Shabbos *kodesh*. I joined in the hustle and bustle of cleaning, showering and dressing up. Friday evening before sunset, I went downstairs with my new friends, impatient for my first meeting with Sarah Schneirer.

The Friday night schedule was more or less as follows:

All the girls would go downstairs to the vestibule — the room leading into the dining hall. A group of girls would go to Sarah Schneirer to call for her and escort her to the seminary, and then together with her we would enter the dining room. Sarah Schneirer would take her place at the head while the rest of us sat on benches on both sides of tables arranged in the form of the letter *ches*. We would all say *Shir Hashirim*, with Sarah Schneirer leading us. For *kabbalas Shabbos* and *Maariv* we walked to the different *shuls* and *shteiblach*.

After *Maariv* we returned to the seminary building for *Kiddush* and the *seudah*. Sarah Schneirer would go home, rejoining us only after she had finished her *seudah* with her family. She would encourage and expect us to prepare *divrei Torah* and would call on anyone who had something to say. I remember getting *divrei Torah* from my father — as did the other girls. Of course she too would add her own comments. After finishing eating and singing *zemiros* we would go up to the "Roiter Zal" (the hall we called the auditorium) to listen to a prepared report by one of the girls on the *parashah* of the week.

Now to go back to my first Friday night at the seminary. I left off when I had been waiting impatiently for my first glimpse of Sarah Schneirer. When at last she entered, escorted by a group of girls, I saw before me an average-looking woman of medium height, with a white lace apron, having the appearance of a typical motherly woman, until I saw her eyes. Those eyes were mild and loving, and yet they shone with a fiery light. Whatever it was that helped make the impression, I — a young New York girl — felt that I was in the presence of a great woman.

The following incident during that first meeting left an indelible impression. I was dressed in a light, sand-colored silky dress, trimmed with white. The sleeves were *tziniusdig* and the hem came down well past my knees. The neckline, too, I thought was proper, but I soon found out that it did not meet the requirements of Sarah Schneirer. She greeted me warmly, in her deep Galician Yiddish. Although I did not understand every word she said, I truly felt welcome. Still smiling, she approached me, took a large pin and pinned up the neckline of my dress, saying something to the effect that in Bais Yaakov we insist on one hundred-percent *tzinius* and cannot compromise in any way whatsoever. Some of the girls — my new friends and protectresses — stood aghast. As for me, oddly enough I felt no resentment or embarrassment. It must have been her unassuming simplicity and obvious sincerity that somehow made her gesture seem both natural and in place. No, I did not feel any embarrassment! I followed her into the room and seated myself at her side to say *Shir Hashirim* for the first time in Cracow.

I'll never forget that first Friday night in Cracow. What a contrast to the Friday nights in New York!

The streets were filled with men, women and children hurrying to the different *shuls* and *shteiblach*. Everyone was dressed in their special Shabbos raiment, the men and boys shining in the special silken *bekeshes* and *shtriemlach*. In the *shteiblach* the singing of *Kabbalas Shabbos* and of *Lecho Dodi* — each stanza with a different melody to fit the text — was full of yearning and gladness. The *lichtigkeit* and the joyous Shabbos *kedushah* was indescribable. How sad, how terribly sad that it is no more.

❦   ❦   ❦

I arrived in Cracow in *Tamuz*. It was a little while before the whole seminary was going to pack up and leave for the mountains for study during the summer. After that all the girls — except for the "Amerikanke" — would travel home for the *Yomim Noraim*. I was going to join my teacher Fraulein Hamburger from Germany for a fascinating journey throughout the great Torah centers of Poland. Succos I was going to spend in Baranovitz with my relatives,

*Wedding
photograph of
Rabbi Chaim Avram
and
Rebbetzin Chava
Pincus*

the Slonimer Rebbe and his family.

There was some time until the seminary would be traveling to the Carpathian Mountains where they would have two months of intensive study. Until then we all went back to class. I was assigned to S-1, the first-year course.

I remember the classroom. It was large, airy, with windows facing the Wisla (the river flowing through Cracow). I chose a seat in the back, near a window, and from that vantage point tried to take in everything: the teachers, my classmates, what was being taught and how. Some of the lectures were in German, which I had never learned. We studied the works of the Shamshon Rafael Hirsch School, with special emphasis on his *Gesamelte Schriften* — all in German. It was in *hoch Deutch* — a difficult, classical German which I did not begin to understand. Even those classes which were conducted in Yiddish were difficult for me to follow. The Yiddish we heard at home was Lithuanian, while in Cracow it was a real deep Galician, but I tried very hard and soon managed well with these languages.

In observing my classmates, there was one girl in particular who caught my attention. She had a little ponytail sticking out, lots of freckles and just couldn't sit still. She was constantly bobbing up and down, asking questions, making comments and, in general making herself heard, much of what she said I did not understand. What an obstreperous girl, I thought to myself, until I got to know her and understand what she had to say. The first time I was impressed with her was when she prepared a lesson in *Pairush Hatefillah* on *Baruch She'amar*. I listened with amazement as this very young girl explained so ably the *tefillah*, clarifying the nuances and deep philosophical meaning of each statement.

I was equally impressed by their knowledge and deep understanding in all the other courses which I attended: *Chumash*, *Neviim*, etc. Another opportunity in which they excelled was on Shabbos *kodesh*. Each girl was assigned a *parashah* on which she was to prepare an address to deliver Friday night after the *seudah* during the winter, or on Shabbos afternoon during the summer months. Most of those presentations were exceptionally well done, very interesting and thought provoking.

For a seminary student the summer months were special in many ways. The girls would pack up and leave for the Carpathian Mountains. Here they enjoyed two summer months devoted to intensive study amid the surroundings of beautiful mountain scenery, seated at rustic tables built under trees. Special guests lecturers would be invited. One of them, whose coming was awaited with much anticipation, was Dr. Shmuel Leo Deutschlander, head of the Bais Yaakov in Vienna. It is hard to describe the personality of this extraordinary man. He was a product of the best of Western culture, combined with a burning love for Torah and for *Klal Yisrael*. This princely, gracious personality would travel from city to city, country to country, speaking to philanthropists, lecturing before audiences and enlisting their support for the Torah centers of Poland. He was behind the "Keren Hatorah" which supported all the Talmud Torahs, *chadarim* and Bais Yaakov schools. He, together with others, whom he had interested, raised the funds for the erection of the modern seminary building in Cracow. For us girls, a lesson from Dr. Deutschlander was an occasion highly prized and cherished. I did not have the *zechus* to hear many of his lectures, but the few I did are precious and unforgettable.

The special "bonus" we had during the summer months — a very important one for me — was the fact that Sarah Schneirer was with us constantly, which gave us an opportunity to be closer to her than we could in Cracow. In the first stage of Bais Yaakov the girls had lived together with Sarah Schneirer. They learned together, ate together, slept with a thin wall dividing them, and so were constantly observing her through direct association. When I came she had married again, a *talmid chacham* by the name of Rabbi Landau, and called herself Sarah Schneirer Landau. We girls were of course living in the dormitory. We saw her in class, except when she was away on behalf of Bais Yaakov. When she returned she would give us an interesting report of each mission. As much, or as little, as we saw of her was very much appreciated, but we did not enjoy the intimacy and closeness that was the fortunate lot of her first *talmidos*.

Tishrei and *Nissan* were two months of vacation for the seminary. All the students traveled home except of course, the "Amerikanke" and Fraulein Hamburger. I was very fortunate to be included in the plans she made to travel and visit all the important and interesting centers of Poland.

We started with Lublin, still managing to see it at the height of its greatness, before the death of the *rosh yeshivah*.

From there we traveled to Warsaw and to Ger. We arrived *erev* Rosh Hashanah in time to witness the stream of thousands and thousands of *chassidim* coming to Ger to spend Rosh Hashanah with the Rebbe. We had the rare honor and privilege of being invited by the Rebbetzin to hear the Rebbe's *Kiddush*. I cannot put into words the feeling of being in the presence of this great leader and *gadol*. It is difficult to describe the holiness that shone from his countenance. We looked out into the courtyard where there were over ten thousand *chassidim* gathered and were awestruck.

Yom Kippur I stayed with the famous Lubavitcher Gurary family whose daughter was a very dear friend of mine. We *davened* at the *beis medrash* of the former Lubavitcher Rebbe, another great leader. My father termed him a great man for his self-sacrifice on behalf of *Klal Yisrael*.

Between Yom Kippur and Succos we visited the famous Mirrer Yeshiva where we were received in the homes of the *rosh yeshivah* and the *mashgiach*. From the famous little *fensterel* on the second floor of the *yeshivah* we looked down into the *beis midrash* and saw hundreds of young men learning and *davening*.

Succos I spent in Baranovitch, where the Slonimer Rebbi, the Rebbetzin and the whole family went out of their way to make me, the daughter of R' Matis, welcome and feel at home. I also spent some time with my unforgettable friend, Rebbetzin Kaplan, then Vichna Eisen. Together we visited and I got to know her aunt and her uncle, R' Yisroel Yaakov, who was the *mashgiach* of the *yeshivah*. I also was privileged to see R' Elchonon. Yes, this one month I managed to see a big portion of the heart of Jewry.

The second *bein hazmanim* in *Chodesh Nissan* I traveled to *Eretz Yisrael*, where my mother and my younger brothers and sisters were. I heard of a special excursion offered by the Agudas Yisrael of Frankfort, Germany. I wrote to ask if I could join. I received a telegram saying that I could join if I would be in Frankfort within twenty-four hours. Well, the whole seminary was excited. They got to work and helped me get there on time. One of the girls ran to obtain the visas I would need; another ran to the attic to get my valises. In short, I was soon packed and on my way and arrived in Frankfort within twenty-four hours. This was 1933. I vividly remember the atmosphere of fear and terror surrounding me. The shutters of buildings were closed; no one moved out of the offices. Still, no one could begin to foresee the horrors that were to come. We quickly left Germany for Switzerland and then on to Italy, where we boarded a ship at Messina. Among the large number of passengers there were many prominent leaders and industrialists. I was fascinated by all I saw and heard. There were many addresses by famous and illustrious personalities. One of the highlights for me was the address of the daughter of R' Yaakov Rosenheim, in which she made an appeal for funds to establish religious kindergartens to be built in *Eretz Yisrael*.

Many of those present were going to explore possibilities of establishing themselves and were planning to remain in *Eretz Yisrael*. In *Eretz Yisrael* I kept in touch with my group. I was told that the famous Dr. Wallach, the religious doctor and founder of Shaarei Zedek hospital, had sixty to seventy people each day as his guests. Quoting the *Chazal* that one should know the people with whom he dines, it was his practice that before the meal each guest would rise and briefly introduce himself, giving his name, where he comes from and any other information that might interest his listeners.

I stayed in *Eretz Yisrael* from *erev* Pesach till before *Lag B'Omer*. Besides the joy of seeing my mother and little brothers and sister, I got to know my big family which I only vaguely remembered from my childhood.

It was very disappointing that the people of *Eretz Yisrael* knew very little of Bais Yaakov, and daughters of even very pious Jews attended schools not of our *hashkafah*. As such, they ridiculed my unusual modest dress and what they called my extreme *"chinyuk- ishe"* way of looking at things. It is interesting to mention that there was one Bais Yaakov school in Tiberias, founded by my uncle, the later Slonimer Rebbe, and supported by *"Eretz Yisrael gelt,"* which my father sent from New York. From among my shipmates, many attempts were made to convince me to remain in *Eretz Yisrael* and not to return to Poland, because they claimed that the *galus* was a sinking ship from which everyone — who could — should escape.

I was still in the seminary when Sarah Schneirer passed away. She suffered a devastating illness and throughout her suffering she never uttered one word of complaint. Up to her last, her thoughts were with her *talmidos* whom she encouraged and inspired. Dr. Deutschlander termed her an *olah temimah* (an unblemished sacrificial offering). I had the *zechus* of seeing her a day before her *petirah*. I broke down at her bedside crying, and I too realized that she was an *olah temimah*. Only her light-filled eyes remained of her. She caressed and comforted me and asked me not to cry, that all is well. The next day, Friday, after she lit the Shabbos candles, she returned her pure soul to her Maker. All of Poland and Jews everywhere to whom Torah was precious mourned this truly great woman.

I will not attempt at this time to describe that which we acquired in Bais Yaakov. I am not referring to the curriculum; that can be easily assembled. More important was the love for, and the appreciation of, all that we learned; the basic *hashkafos* and the great horizons that were revealed to us as daughters and teachers of our people, and, eventually, as mothers and builders of *Bais Yisrael*. Bais Yaakov in Cracow was an important part of the "workshop for the *nitzchius*, the eternity, of our people."

I left Poland for New York after Sarah Schneirer's *petirah*.

I hope, I dream, that with the help of *Hakadosh Baruch Hu* I may be privileged some day to describe in part what Bais Yaakov was, and what it has meant both to me personally and to the generations of *Klal Yisrael*.

An Insight into Sarah Schneirer

y father praised her as a *yarei shamayim*, and he considered that the greatest praise one could give a person. Sarah Schneirer had, I think, this attribute which is the most difficult to achieve in a truly great measure.

I will not dwell upon what her *talmidos* saw in her everyday life which so enriched us, but I will mention several insights into her truly remarkable character.

First and foremost: her absolute *yiras Hashem* and *ahavas Hashem* which, in turn, led to her single-minded love for Torah and *bnei Yisrael*. I don't remember actually hearing this parable from her, but I absorbed its lesson into my very being. If you would see a Jewish child lying faint, naked and hungry, a child so terribly deprived, you would instinctively want to take him into your arms, feed and clothe him. A Jewish child who did not receive a Torah-true education was considered by Sarah Schneirer truly deprived, even more so than the child described above. In the former case it is the body that is suffering, but when he has no Torah education it is the *neshamah* which is starving. She felt, and managed to convey this feeling to her *talmidos*, that it was our privilege and responsibility to reach such Jewish children and bring them to, what she called, a "*chaim*-true" life.

It was her courage and idealism that made her pick up the rocks thrown at her by violent opponents to Bais Yaakov. Rocks in hand, she would turn to her *talmidos* saying, "We will take these rocks and turn them into bricks with which we will build Bais Yaakov." And she did just that.

She was a rare mixture of extraordinary *Yiddishe shtolz* — Jewish pride — on the one hand, and her *tznius* and *anivus* — modesty and humility — on the other.

Imagine! The cornerstone of the Bais Yaakov Seminary building in Cracow was to be laid. The leaders of Jewry were there, important personalities of the Torah world and the communal world, writers, thinkers and a great crowd of ordinary people, all gathered together to participate in this event. It was a real celebration with music, a band playing and speakers being called upon to address the crowd.

Amidst this celebration and gaiety, where was Sarah Schneirer, the founder and inspiration of all this? She was standing at the far end of the crowd, together with the women, her friends and neighbors, shedding tears and whispering her prayer: "Please, *Hakadosh Baruch Hu*, now that we are about to have our own modern building with all the conveniences, and now that we are to acquire the latest pedagogical educational system, watch over us, please, *Hashem*, that all this affluence does not affect us. Help us so that we do not, *chas v'shalom* (Heaven forbid), forget the purpose of Bais Yaakov. Help us remember always that we are here to serve You and to educate the future generations to learn Torah and carry out *mitzvos*."

Her Yiddishe Shtolz

fter the first few years of the existence of Bais Yaakov, there arose a very serious problem. Parents began to appreciate what Sarah Schneirer was accomplishing with her *talmidos* and they came to her asking that she help them build Bais Yaakov schools in their respective towns and cities. If there were to be schools, there must be teachers. Trained teachers she did not as yet have. The first girls with whom she started seven or eight years before were only six or seven years old then; now, they were thirteen or fourteen.

But the schools were springing up, schools which could not function without teachers. Some of these young fourteen-year-old girls, who later became teachers in the Bais Yaakov Seminary and leaders of the movement, would laughingly remember and relate how they solved this problem. They would "put up their hair," put on high-heeled shoes and adapt very grown-up expressions to seem the mature teachers they were supposed to be.

Even before this problem arose, when her one little group grew into many classes, Sarah Schneirer could not possibly teach them all by herself. Her first disciples would later describe how Sarah Schneirer prepared them to teach the younger classes. She filled notebook after notebook with notes on different subjects. At night she would prepare the lesson for each "assistant teacher" to relay to her charges the next morning. These notebooks were cherished by the "student" teachers and served them in good stead later when they were brave enough to assume regular posts and become full-fledged teachers and leaders of their schools.

I saw some of these notebooks. Some of the lessons would be in the form of questions and answers. For example:

> Question: In what does a Jewish girl take pride?
>
> Answer: A Jewish girl is proud that she is part of the Jewish people. Because we are the children of the Patriarchs: Avraham, Yitzchak and Yaakov. Because we are the children of the Matriarchs: Sarah, Rivkah, Rachel and Leah. We are also proud that *Hashem* has chosen us as the treasured nation, and has given us the Holy Torah.

These questions would be read out loud and each little girl would rise and in a loud voice filled with pride would give the proper answer.

It was these Torah *yesodos* and *hashkafos* which they had absorbed in their training that they passed on in due time to their pupils.

Another example of her *Yiddishe shtolz*: unshakeable belief in and pride of every *din*. It is related that at one of the public meetings, a personality of the secular world offered his hand to Sarah Schneirer and she, of course, explained that she was not permitted by Jewish law to take it. He made a remark to the effect that he was sure that she was quite unique and that she was probably the only one in all of Poland — and maybe in the world — to act this way. She answered: "Perhaps at present, but not for long. Soon there will be a whole generation of thousands of knowledgeable girls who will know the *halachah* and adhere to it."

Her Way of Doing Mitzvos

hatever Sarah Schneirer did was done with her whole being. Once she considered a matter important she would not rest until she saw it through. She felt that it was of ultimate importance that our girls, the future mothers of *Klal Yisrael*, should speak Yiddish. It was the language in which *gedolei hador*, both past and present, wrote and taught. Next to *lashon kodesh*, it was our language.

The girls, especially those in Cracow, were always chatting in Polish, as we in the United States do in English. Sarah Schneirer explained, appealed, requested and reminded, and after that she could also raise her voice and speak angrily, trying to enforce the importance of speaking Yiddish. When she was in the hospital, she wrote to Reb Yehuda Leib Orlean to tell her beloved *talmidos* that by making an effort to talk Yiddish they would afford her great pleasure and *nachas ruach*.

Tzedakah and *chessed* were an integral part of her life all year round and especially during the months of *Nissan* and *Tishrei* when the seminary was closed. In the then-poverty-stricken Cracow she unassumingly and quietly collected thousands of *zlotys*, providing regular stipends to needy families and helping to marry off their children.

She drew us, her *talmidos*, into her *chessed* acts. I remember having a little notebook with the addresses of people who pledged a certain weekly sum for Sarah Schneirer's charities. On Friday afternoon I would climb up tenement staircases to collect ... I can't believe it, but I think it was twenty *groschen* per family. The exchange rate was five *zlotys* per dollar, which means that each *zloty* was worth twenty cents. One hundred *groschen* was worth one *zloty*, which means that five *groschen* were worth one cent. Thus we walked from door to door, up stairs, down stairs, to collect four cents from a family! This may give you an idea of the poverty of *bnei Yisrael* then in Poland.

Her Yiras Shamayim

 part of *Chodesh Nissan* of one year I spent in Cracow. Before Pesach, I, together with one of the Bnos girls, helped Sarah Schneirer with *bedikas chametz* (searching for leaven). To observe Sarah Schneirer at *bedikas chametz* in the seminary was an experience. It was observing a real *avodas Hashem*. She spent hours going through each desk and each closet. It was quite a job just holding a candle for her as she put in real work checking each desk and, if necessary, cleaning or wiping up those that were not done at all or not done to her satisfaction. Her intense and devoted attention at *bedikas chametz* could serve as a lesson on how to perform a *mitzvah* with *shlaimus*.

The last point I want to mention can be illustrated in the following way. It is Shabbos, late afternoon. We are at a *shalosh seudos* in the Bais Yaakov Seminary of Williamsburg. The seminary lights did not go on. We are absorbed talking about Bais Yaakov and my experiences in Cracow.

Years later, one of those students approached me and reminded me of that particular talk. "We heard so much about the ideals of Bais Yaakov, the love of learning and the importance of *chessed*, but I cannot tell you how much I got and how much I appreciated what you told us then. You described the happy moments in Bais Yaakov, the interesting and beautiful trips you went on which lasted two or three days at a time. You spoke about the many hours of dancing and singing to the tune of *Vetaher Libeinu*. You told us about Purim celebrations when the girls showed how gifted they were and what a sense of humor they possessed by the *grammen* they prepared poking fun at life in the seminary.

"Then you described an outing you had. How your class, together with Sarah Schneirer, walked through a thick forest during a good part of the night, planning to climb to the top of one of the tallest Carpathian Mountains and to reach it in time to see the sunrise. With guides leading you, you got there just in time. You were all seated around, Sarah Schneirer looking towards the east as the sun began to rise. We felt the awe and wonder you experienced as you observed the awesome might and beauty of *Hashem's* world. Then Sarah Schneirer whispered: השמים מספרים כבוד א-ל ומעשי ידיו מגיד הרקיע — *The heavens declare the glory of Hashem, and the expanse of the sky tells of His handiwork.*

One of the *maspidim* (speakers), after her *petirah* (passing), described her life as a program — a complete plan for attaining *shlaimus* (greatness).

The Torah, of course, is the ultimate "blueprint" for perfection. There are *sefarim*, many classics with detailed instructions of step-by-step striving for perfection. We are told that chapter 119 in *Tehillim*, if studied carefully and followed, will help us in this endeavor, and so will Chapter 145.

Sarah Schneirer had her own simplified plan that helped her reach perfection (as much as can be attained by a human being). She chose several verses in *Tehillim* which she taught, reviewed, and taught again, meditated upon and delved into. They were printed, posted and decorated every classroom of every Bais Yaakov and in meeting rooms of Bnos and Neshei. The smallest child from kindergarten throughout school and on to adulthood knew them and understood their meaning. I will mention only a few.

שויתי ה' לנגדי תמיד. The little girls would stand up and proudly recite the verse with the Yiddish translation: איך זעה הקב"ה פאר מיר תמיד. ער זעהט אלץ וואס איך טוא: ער הערט אלץ וואס איך רעד (ער וויסט אלץ וואס איך טראכט), און ער שרייבט אלץ אריין אין א בוך. — I see Hashem before me always; He sees everything I do; hears everything I say; (knows everything I think,) and writes everything in a book.

From very young childhood they were taught that one should not lie, steal, hurt or mislead anyone ... Why? Not because she'll be found out or punished or disgraced. But because Hashem said so. Hakadosh Baruch Hu is before us always; there's no hiding from Him. Sarah Schneirer illustrated this in her daily life. We felt that there was not a moment when she did not remember and was not conscious of the fact that she was in the presence of Hakadosh Baruch Hu.

Another favorite verse was: למנות ימינו כן הודע — Help us count our days. She would explain with simple parables that in order for a day to be considered and counted as a day of life, it must be filled with Torah and mitzvos. A day which is spent in eating, sleeping, small talk, etc., is a day of "existence" — not of life. That's how animals live — they exist, perish and return to nothingness. We, Knesses Yisrael, know that this world is for accomplishment. רצה הקב"ה לזכות את ישראל לפיכך הרבה להם תורה ומצוות — Torah and mitzvos were given to purify us, to elevate us to perfection. We must strive to make each day count as a day of life.

Another verse: וטהר לבנו לעבדך באמת. We pray to Hashem: Help us to have pure hearts so we can serve You b'emes, with sincerity. Tefillah, prayer, was one of the pillars through which she reached up. What she expected of us was that we say each word of prayer clearly, that we try to understand and meditate upon its meaning. This was sure to make us feel closer to Hashem and was bound to help us attain the attributes we sought.

And this final verse: עבדו את ה' בשמחה — Serve Hashem with gladness. Hakadosh Baruch Hu created this world in order to do chessed with His creation. We must try to see and to appreciate the goodness and sweetness of *Hashem's* world and after enjoying it, we must express our thanks. She would add that just as we accept blessings with joy, so too must we try to accept hardships, for whatever *Hashem* does is good.

I mentioned earlier the special "bonus" we had in having Sarah Schneirer with us during the summer months. There we would not only be in class with her, but we would take walks together. Sometimes we would hire a wagon — a simple farmer's cart — and go on an outing to one of the villages where our people were established. And so had opportunities to listen ... and learn. We would be riding up a hill when she would call out to us: "זעהט קינדער — Look, my children, see how difficult it is to go up! To climb up is not easy... but (as we went down hill) — see how easy it is to go down, to fall ... "

We would pass railroad tracks. "Look — when the trains start out to an important destination and ride together on a straight line, towards the same goal, they will both get there. Should, however, one stray or deviate even the slightest from the straight path, there's no telling where it will end up.

She would tell us of the disciple who came to his Rebbe. "Rebbe, איך האב אויסגעלערנט גאנץ ש"ס — *I have learned the entire Talmud.*"

"Hmm, is that so?" said his Rebbe, "וואס האט ש"ס דיר אויסגעלערנט — *What did the Talmud teach you?*"

We knew that Sarah Schneirer was not telling us just stories or parables. She was speaking about יהדות, the meaning and purpose of life. Don't let yourself be distracted from what is right, don't deviate in any way. It's laborious climbing, but it's worth it, for you will live these precious years *Hakadosh Baruch Hu* grants you, to the fullest, most enjoyable and most enriching way.

Sarah Schneirer strove for *shlaimus*, not just for herself but for all her *talmidos* — for all of *Klal Yisrael*. A very important tribute to her greatness was the greatness of her *talmidos*. She imbued them with her own love of *Hakadosh Baruch Hu*, His Torah and with the will power to continue her work and to pass on this reaching out for *shlaimus* to the coming generations.

The story of Sarah Schneirer would not be complete without mentioning her greatest *talmidah* — Rebbetzin Vichna Kaplan (Vichna Eisen, as she was then known).

Vichna was in the second-year seminary when I arrived in Cracow and she became one of my dearest friends. I already perceived in her then unusual talents, both spiritual and intellectual. The times I spent with her are full of interesting and even humorous experiences, one of which I'll mention here.

We were together in Baranovitz where she lived with her aunt and uncle, Reb Yisrael Yaakov, who was the *mashgiach* of the *yeshivah* in Baranowitz, and where I visited with my relatives, the Rebbe of Slonim and his family. It was a small town which was then still without a Bais Yaakov school and needed much influencing to get the people to build one. Vichna took advantage of the presence of our teacher, Miss Hamburger, and myself, and planned a huge mass meeting in order to impress the people with the importance and attainments of Bais Yaakov. There were posters and leaflets all over Baranovitz announcing the event and featuring Fraulein Hamburger as the main speaker. Vichna also drafted me, the little greenhorn "Amerikanke" — just a few weeks from America — to speak before the huge crowd. Of course, I flatly refused, but there was no refusing Vichna, so I found myself on the podium. I cannot recall in which language I spoke — it must have been Yiddish — and I don't know how much they understood. However, what was most clear to them was that someone traveled all the way from New York to study in Bais Yaakov with Sarah Schneirer, and that in America and other parts of the world Jews were inspired by the accomplishments of Bais Yaakov and were hoping that the *chinuch* and the ideology of Bais Yaakov would become available to their daughters in America and the world over. I cannot recall many details of the meeting, but I do remember the enthusiasm and warm response on the part of the huge assemblage.

Vichna was already then concerned with the need to help every Jewish child obtain a Torah-true education. She followed the *derech* of our great teacher, in that she strived for *shlaimus*, not only for herself but for *Klal Yisrael*.

Epilogue

he great *talmidos* of Sarah Schneirer numbered in the many many thousands. I'm referring not only to those who were leaders of the Bais Yaakov movement and teachers in the Bais Yaakov Seminary. I'm referring to all the Sarahs and Rachels, the Rivkies and Feigies, to their pure faith and love for *Hashem*, all who gave up their lives for *kiddush Hashem*.

The *hashgachah*, with much compassion, made possible the escape from the destruction of a few of her *talmidos* for the task to rebuild Bais Yaakov in America and in the world over.

Rebbetzin Vichna Kaplan, one of the greatest of her *talmidos*, arrived on our shores in 1937. She continued to build in the United States what Sarah Schneirer built in Poland. She emulated her in every way.

Rebbetzin Basya Bender arrived in 1939. Later followed Rebbetzin Chava Wachtfogel, Rivka Springer, Chana Rottenberg, Rochel Cizner, Shifra Yudasin, Bat-Sheva Hutner and Leah Goldstein.

Together we were destined to work together to build Bais Yaakov in America and make it the world movement it is today, a blessing and spiritual growth and renewal for *Klal Yisrael*.

Impressions of
an American Visitor

by Rebbetzin Chava (Gordon) Schechter

t happened in the year 1933. I had decided that summer to spend my month's vacation abroad instead of at an adult camp somewhere in the Catskill Mountains. My motive for such a trip was twofold: (a) to visit my brother who was learning in the Yeshiva in Mir, Poland and whom I had not seen for four years, and (b) to visit my friend, Chava Weinberg, who was spending her second year of study at the Bais Yaakov Seminary in Cracow. At that time there were numerous American *yeshivah bachurim* who had left home to pursue their learning in the great *yeshivos* of Eastern Europe, but for an American girl to have the courage and spiritual urge to take such a "giant step" was unheard of. I, for one, had never heard of the existence of such a school or the name of Sarah Schneirer. I was, therefore, very curious to see for myself what was the attraction for an American girl in Cracow.

Before arriving in Cracow I had gathered a few statistics on the Bais Yaakov movement in general. They had by 1933 — much to my surprise — a network of two hundred elementary schools throughout Poland, with a total registration of about thirty thousand students. The teachers for these schools were being trained at the seminary in Cracow where they occupied a new five-story building, fully equipped with classrooms, an auditorium , a dining hall and dormitory. When I came there I found one hundred and twenty resident students between the ages of sixteen and twenty. Only six of the women were from Cracow and the rest from neighboring cities and distant towns, and our one and only American.

One summer, an American, Chava Gordon, came to Cracow for a visit. These are her impressions of her stay there. Today, she lives in *Eretz Yisrael* with her husband, Rabbi Shechter.

My friend, Chava, received permission for me to move into the dormitory, attend classes together with her and participate in all the seminary activities. Suffice it to say that after my first Shabbos I took the liberty of sending a cable to my boss that I was extending my vacation for another month. I figured to remain until the seminary girls went home to spend the *Yomim Tovim* with their families, and during that time I would go to the Mirrer Yeshiva to visit my brother. What follows are my impressions of that memorable visit in Cracow.

A regular weekday schedule proceeded along the following lines:

6:00 a.m. — Dressed, *davened*, and reviewed lessons.
7:45 — Breakfast: cup of cocoa, bread and butter.
8:00-9:30 — First Period — *Chumash*.

How different in that class was the interpretation of the verse from *Ha'azinu* from what I had heard from my schoolteacher in the States! ימצאהו בארץ מדבר ובתהו ילל ישימון, יסבבנהו יבוננהו יצרנהו כאישון עינו Long before the Jewish people had a land of its own it was formed into a nation. *Hashem* found them in the desert and that is where He molded them into a nation. *Klal Yisrael* became a nation, not by virtue of its land and language, but through receiving the Torah in the desert.

9:30-11:00 — *Shir Hashirim*.

From the way I was taught this *Megillah* back home I wondered how it came to be included in the *Kisvai HaKodesh*. But here I began to understand the words of Rabbi Akiva: "No day is as important as the day *Shir Hashirim* was given to Israel, for all the Scriptures are Holy, but *Shir Hashirim* is Holy of Holies. It is a song expressing sentiments of eager yearning and mutual love between *Hashem* and *Knesses Yisrael*, and *Ahavas Yisrael* by *Hakadosh Baruch Hu* — this and only this is true love, and has meaning and value only insofar as the degree of *Ahavas Hashem* is involved in that love. That is the kind of love that Rabbi Akiva himself had for his wife who gave him the courage to begin learning at the age of forty, and the perseverance to continue to become the great Rabbi Akiva.

11:00-11:30 — Intermission for mid-morning snack.
11:30- 1:00 — History.

Learned about the rise of the Reform movement and the important role played by Rabbi Shamshon Rafael Hirsch in stemming the tide of assimilation.

1:00 - 2:00 — *Dinim*.

I have a vivid recollection of a slaughtered chicken that was brought into the classroom to demonstrate the difference between a chicken that is kosher or *treif*.

2:00 - 3:00 — Lunch.

The first day I ate the *kashe* but left over the soup and was severely reprimanded for transgressing בל תשחית (wasting food). The outstanding feature of this hour was the digest of the news of the day presented by a different student each week. After lunch we usually went for a walk.

3:30 - 4:00 — *Minchah*.
4:00 - 4:30 — Tea.
4:30 - 7:30 — Study, homework, recopying of notes taken in class.
7:30 - 8:00 — *Maariv*.
8:00 - 9:00 — Supper.
9:00 -10:00 — Informal reading group.

Miss G. (one of the teachers) read a few chapters from the *sefer* תנאי הנפש בחסדות and the girls took an active part in the discussion. I was impressed by their profound knowledge and ability to express views and opinions on a subject matter which was sometimes much beyond my comprehension.

10:00 — And so to bed. All lights out.

During my first week at the school I heard constant reference to the name "Frau Schneirer." When I had arrived she was out-of-town on one of her regular trips, addressing mass meetings, organizing schools or lending assistance and encouragement to some of the out-of-town alumnae. I could hardly wait till *Erev Shabbos*, when she was expected back. After the candles were lit, everybody was standing around waiting. My curiosity was at its height. Then the long-awaited moment arrived. The door opened; Frau Schneirer entered. She was very simply dressed and made a very modest appearance. What impressed me most at the moment was not so much the woman who was standing before me, but the change in the room that had come about by her mere presence. It seemed so different with her here, an inexplicable something that added to the *kedushah* of Shabbos. The girls circled about her, stood with awe and reverence before her, ever ready to serve and obey as a *chassid* his *rebbe*.

I took advantage of her presence that Friday night to follow her wherever I could. After *Maariv* I joined a few girls who escorted her home. On the way she turned the conversation to thoughts on the *sedrah* of the week or some story of *gadlus Hashem*. Her favorite one seemed to be that of the atheist who told her that he does not believe in G-d. "Why not?" she asked. "Because I do not believe in what I cannot see." "Do you believe in Napoleon?" she asked. "Of course I do," was his quick rejoinder. To which she replied: "Have you ever seen Napoleon?"

The more I observed her — even though it was only for a short period — the more I realized her greatness from her dedicated love of true *Yiddishkeit*, her warmth and compassion, and the תורת חסד על לשונה, Torah of kindness was always on her lips. But above all, her greatness was manifested in her *tzinius*. Her great qualities stemmed from this all-encompassing *middah*. It permeated and enveloped everything she did in her service to the *Ribbono Shel Olam* and in her dedication to *Klal Yisrael*.

Twice during her two years' stay at the seminary, each student was given the opportunity to address the entire student body and faculty. She took her stand on the platform and with poise and fluency delivered her *drashah* (speech). It had as its theme an idea culled from the *sedrah* of the week and into it was woven much of the knowledge and information that had been gleaned from *sifrei chazal* (writings of our sages) and commentators and the various courses studied during the year. A great deal of time and preparation was put into its composition, each girl knowing weeks in advance the date when she would be scheduled to speak. Following this "referat" by a student of the graduating class, the second "referat", based on the *haftorah*, was delivered by an undergraduate. Each *drashah* lasted from one half to one hour. This was followed by the *seudah shlishis*, *Maariv* and *Havdalah* — and in between they sang and danced and there was general rejoicing.

The only time I found these girls saddened and depressed was on the last day of school. The thought of graduation and the return home meant for them not so much a day of celebration and happiness at the attainment of a goal, but sorrow and regret at the thought of having to part and separate from teachers and classmates. For two years they had lived in a utopian peace and harmony and now they had to go out and face reality, become teachers in some distant province where all alone they would have to contend with opposition. In union there is strength, but now that they had to separate, the ordeal became so much more trying.

As far as I can recall, I think I went away from that graduation with a feeling of deep concern for the girls over the important mission they were about to embark upon. There was no doubt in my mind, however, that they would succeed in their *shlichus* (mission).

And why not? Their fear and apprehension at accepting a job out-of-town would soon be allayed by virtue of their *mesiras nefesh* for spreading *Yiddishkeit* in the provinces. The difficulties they would face, because of their being young and inexperienced, would not discourage them by virtue of their deep pride in their heritage and their strong *hashkafos*. And last but not least, their *yiras shamayim* and dedication to the cause of Bais Yaakov would give them the self-confidence required to meet the challenges of the outside world.

Rebbetzin Vichna Kaplan

Slonim, Russia — 1913

eb Ephraim Yehoshua Eisen and his wife Mereh Gittel rejoiced in the birth of their new baby girl, Vichna, though they could little guess that the small flame that lit up the Eisen household would one day provide a beacon of light for *bnos Yisrael*.

The child enjoyed a calm and peaceful childhood that was abruptly ended with the death of her parents when she was eleven. She and her brother Dovid were taken in by their aunt and uncle. The famed *mashgiach* of Baranovitch, Reb Yisrael Yaakov Lubchansky, and his wife had been childless after several years of marriage. They were happy to open their home to their niece and nephew.

Baranovitch, Poland — 1924

here was no Bais Yaakov or Jewish schools for girls in the *shtetl* of Baranovitch. The more modern parents sent their daughters to public school and then on to gymnasium. The only other alternative was for a group of girls to hire a tutor, as the cost of a private tutor was prohibitive. For many years a man named Meslevsky tutored a small group of girls from the more observant homes, young Vichna Eisen among them.

Vichna possessed an inquisitive mind and knew she could not be content unless she was learning. She had heard of the famed Bais Yaakov of Cracow and, at the age of sixteen, decided to attend. There she could study together with girls her own age who shared her beliefs. Her application to the seminary was rejected, however, because acceptance required a high-school diploma. "Of what consequence is a secular diploma for a girl attending a religious school?" was her immediate reply. The response was sympathetic but firm. Because of the large number of applicants, the administra-

Vichna Eisen at age sixteen

tion needed some way to eliminate candidates, and therefore the criteria of a diploma had been established. And yet, Sarah Schneirer agreed to make an exception. If Vichna could supply proof that she had passed five high-school classes, that would be sufficient. Sure enough, Vichna arranged to pass these classes and eventually was accepted.

Cracow, Poland — 1930

uring her years in Cracow, Vichna was always the top student in her class. After a short time her potential as an assistant to Sarah Schneirer began to surface, and she began to help her in a variety of ways. It was Vichna who went from door to door collecting for Sarah Schneirer's special fund for poor families.

She had an exceptional mind and a wide breadth of knowledge. Everyone marveled at her unique ability to repeat a class or speech verbatim. When she spoke at assemblies, her audience was spellbound by her presence and intelligence.

As time passed it became obvious that Vichna was Frau Schneirer's closest pupil, and yet no one was jealous. Everyone recognized that somehow she had earned that special relationship.

The night of graduation was one etched in the minds of those present. Not all of the original one hundred and fifty students who had begun the course remained, but the crowd was still impressive — impressive in its *achdus* (unity), impressive in its spirit, impressive in all its members had accomplished. Sarah Schneirer was in her element. The joy she had in seeing the girls she had molded turn into mature young ladies ready to teach the children of *Klal Yisrael* was boundless. They danced and sang all night, to the tune of *v'taher libeinu* echoing through the building.

Shortly thereafter, Vichna and her former classmates were told where they would be teaching. Her life as a *mechanechess* (teacher) was about to begin.

Brisk, Poland

he situation in the Bais Yaakov in Brisk was similar to that of many towns in Poland. The school was small and Fraulein Eisen was the only teacher of Jewish subjects. She immersed herself in her job, spending all her time preparing and creating lessons to interest her pupils. She even spent Shabbos together with her students. After candle lighting on Friday night, they crowded into Fraulein Eisen's apartment. The girls sat mesmerized as she told story after story until their fathers came to pick them up after *Maariv*. Shabbos afternoons, she helped out with the Basya (Bnos Agudas Yisrael) groups, seeing that everything ran smoothly and in the spirit of Torah.

She left an indelible mark on the town of Brisk. The Brisker Rav himself reiterated his praise of her work and her character. And yet this was only the beginning of what she was to accomplish.

After several years in Brisk she became engaged to Reb Boruch Kaplan, a promising young *bachur* from Mirrer Yeshiva. They made plans to settle in America, where he had grown up.

Before leaving Poland, Fraulein Eisen asked Reb Yehuda Leib Orlean, *menahel* of the Cracow Seminary, for permission to start a

Bais Yaakov school in America. Even at this important moment in her life, Bais Yaakov was uppermost in her mind.

Leaving behind all her family and friends, Vichna Eisen sailed to America to become Rebbetzin Kaplan. Their wedding was held in the lunch room of the Yeshiva Torah Vodaath where Reb Boruch later became a *maggid shiur* (lecturer).

Williamsburg, New York — 1937

I t was the beginning of a new year, the beginning of the Kaplan home and the beginning of Bais Yaakov in America.

The challenges that young Rebbetzin Kaplan faced differed remarkably from those of her mentor, Sarah Schneirer. Here, the enemy was indifference to Judaism itself. As their boats docked in New York harbor, the Jewish immigrants leading lives of poverty and persecution in Eastern Europe found themselves in a new and startling environment. Arriving with little more than a grim determination to make good, they soon found that "streets paved with gold" were closed to Sabbath-observing Jews. "If you can't come in on Saturday, don't bother coming on Monday." How often they heard the foreman's words; how often they heeded his intractable demand for working on Shabbos.

They worked on Shabbos — it was a necessity, practically *pikuach nefesh*, they reasoned. And then, exhausted by sweatshop routine, they began to miss *minyan*. And, sometimes slowly, and sometimes with stunning swiftness, Judaism was relegated to a little vague knowledge, some holiday foods and perhaps membership in a synagogue visited three times a year.

A Bais Yaakov school in such an environment? The idea was greeted with distrust and suspicion. Even those who clung to their beliefs were wary: Our children must grow up educated, they must become successful professional men and women, they must escape the poverty of Henry Street. Granted, a little *davening*, a bit of *Chumash* knowledge would be nice, but not at the expense of living the American dream!

And yet there were those who were more receptive, who were willing to "risk" their girls in Rebbetzin Kaplan's experiment. In the beginning, seven girls met to study around the dining-room table

A group of Bais Yaakov girls in front of the South Eighth St. building

of the Kaplan home. Evening classes were begun for public high school students and a seminary was founded for older girls. Word spread; students arrived from the five boroughs of New York. The school outgrew its tiny apartment home; classrooms were rented on Keap Street.

Finally, in 1944, the first all-day Bais Yaakov school was begun. In September of 1945, the old army building on South Eighth Street became a school building, and something more: It became a home for students from all over the country, all over the world.

❧ ❧ ❧

Bais Yaakov catered to girls from diverse backgrounds and situations. Naturally, there were the girls from New York and the surrounding areas. Some were local girls from observant families, children of parents who were searching for just this place. Others traveled from neighborhoods as far as an hour away, sometimes against the will of their parents, to attend.

As the school expanded, so did the dormitory. Who were the "out-of-towners" who began to come to Bais Yaakov? Many were daughters of *rabbonim* who had *shuls* in small, obscure towns. These girls felt a kinship to each other, a common background because "the *rav's* daughter" had to act differently. Others came from homes of *frum* Jews who had somehow strayed from New York City, then the center of Orthodox Jewish life in America.

These girls became united by common goals and aspirations, through the teachings of Rebbetzin Kaplan. They loved this vibrant young woman who brought them together, who made them feel proud of being a *bas Yisrael*, who made them want to give over what they had learned.

The building itself was large and impressive, with offices and a library on its first floor, classrooms on its second and, on the top, five rooms tenanted by more than fifty girls. It was here, in the dormitory, that some of Bais Yaakov's greatest lessons were taught.

❧ ❧ ❧

Rebbetzin Kaplan was not only principal of Bais Yaakov Seminary and High School; she established school policies, and personally taught many classes. Her students sat spellbound as they listened to her soothing voice speak of the wonders of *Chumash*, the wisdom of *Mishlei*. She spoke Hebrew fluently and conducted most of her classes in that language. They, her students, were also a part of her private life, baby-sitting when it was necessary or helping her when she needed it.

She herself was always involved with the personal problems of the girls, particularly those in the dorms. They had weekly, sometimes daily, dormitory meetings, where they discussed everything from lack of heat to lack of an ironing board. Nothing was too trivial a problem to discuss with Rebbetzin Kaplan. Somehow, the busy mother, teacher, principal also managed to be *mashgiach* over each and every girl.

Much of what they learned from Rebbetzin Kaplan came from observation. She never lifted her voice and yet she always had perfect control and discipline. Every action she did was thoroughly thought out so as not to inadvertently hurt or offend anyone. This precision of action could be seen even in such everyday things as her handwriting. The perfectly formed letters, written neatly and beautifully, gave much insight into her personality.

Yet all the gentleness, all the calmness was thrown away when a question of *chinuch* or *hashkafah* arose. The famous "Mr. Cohen Story" is a perfect example.

Mr. Cohen was a very wealthy man who wanted to help Bais Yaakov. However, he would not give money to the school for

A group of Bais Yaakov girls in their new uniforms

them to do as they wished. He would choose a specific thing he wanted to provide and that he would buy. First he equipped the auditorium with brand-new theater chairs. Then he ordered custom-made uniforms for all the students.

One day Rebbetzin Kaplan called an emergency assembly in the auditorium. She began talking about all the new luxuries they had been getting. As long as they were acceptable to her she was willing to take them. However, something happened to change all this. Mr. Cohen wanted to hire teachers to teach the girls the art of putting on make-up, fixing hair and, generally, how to be modern young women. This was unacceptable. A school teaching Torah *hashkafah* was not going to teach girls to be modern young ladies. When there is a question of *halachah* or *hashkafah*, there is no compromising. Mr. Cohen was sent packing and the girls learned a lesson they would never forget.

Rebbetzin Kaplan was always in control of every situation, from a very funny incident to a very serious one.

One dark, dreary, rainy night, Rebbetzin Kaplan was in her usual position behind the desk in front of her class teaching *yahadus*. The dormitory supervisor was waiting to lock up after classes ended. She

An ironing board often became the dormitory's "Shabbos tisch"

stood patiently while Rebbetzin Kaplan finished her class and then entered another room for a short teachers' meeting. From her vantage point she saw Rebbetzin Kaplan open the desk drawer to get something. Out jumped a furry cat right into her lap. She looked at the cat with surprise and said, "*Ah chutzpanik!*"

That cat jumped right off and ran out as fast as he could!

Ever so calm, she got up from her desk and adjourned the meeting. Everyone except the dormitory girls had left and it was time to lock the building.

"One minute," said Rebbetzin Kaplan, "I have to make a telephone call."

Five minutes later a taxi arrived and an hour later she had a baby. All this without a change in her gentle, calm, efficient manner.

❀ ❀ ❀

Bais Yaakov played a large role in helping girls who were stranded in post-war Europe, arranging for much-needed supplies, particularly the newly discovered penicillin, to be sent to war-ravaged countries. And as the refugees, so many of them orphaned, began to

Packing to go home

enter the country, they found a home, and a family, in the Bais
Yaakov dormitory. When they were met at Ellis Island, many of the
young girls bore tattoos on their arms and scars on their souls. They
saw the showers of the dormitory and flinched; they had to be
persuaded that all that came out of the faucets was water. They
would wake up fearful and sobbing, and find a comforting hand to
soothe them.

And when these refugees, or any poor student, found a *shidduch*,
it was Bais Yaakov itself that "catered" the wedding, with students
stuffing the celery, cooking the chickens, baking the cakes, taking
the pictures. If necessary, Rebbetzin Kaplan would tell the girls to
help stock the newlyweds' apartment.

❀   ❀   ❀

Although Bais Yaakov was gaining popularity, there were still
some very observant families who did not believe in teaching girls
limudei kodesh. Yet Bais Yaakov was important to them in a
different way. By state law they were required to send their children
to school. These parents sent their girls to Bais Yaakov only for
English subjects and not for *limudei kodesh*.

❀   ❀   ❀

Amid the fun, learning and friendships, there were many
difficulties the girls had to live with. Many were from poor families

who could not afford full tuition or even part. Despite all of their fund-raising efforts, the school had to scrape to get by.

Because of its precarious financial situation, the school was often without heat, and the girls would sleep in sweaters, coats and mittens. One morning, when the cold was so bitter that the water for *negel vasser* had frozen in its container, the girls refused to get out of bed.

Word reached Rebbetzin Kaplan that none of the dormitory girls were in class. She came upstairs and immediately called one of her famous dormitory meetings. In her calm, soothing manner she spoke to them, smoothing out the difficulties. No, they did not get heat, but after Rebbetzin Kaplan's talk it no longer seemed to matter as much.

When the time came for the girls to go home, Rebbetzin Kaplan always called a special meeting.

"Girls," she said, "I know that sometimes school is difficult but if you tell your parents this, they won't send you back. You must always talk positive."

Despite the difficulties and occasional homesickness, all the girls wanted to return to Bais Yaakov. They craved the friendships and learning they could only get in Bais Yaakov. So they closed their mouths and talked only about the good times, keeping the negative parts secret among themselves.

And so the years passed, with a Bais Yaakov education becoming more and more a way of life for religious Jewish girls. The school flourished in Williamsburg, and in 1958 another branch was opened for the growing neighborhood of Boro Park, a branch that eventually supplanted the Williamsburg school. Ten years later, the first full-day intensive-seminary program was begun. And during the years of unprecedented growth, guiding with a tender but firm hand was Rebbetzin Kaplan.

Boro Park — August 1986

n August of 1986, the flame that lit up the Eisen household for over seventy years was extinguished. The hundreds of thousands who felt the effect of her warmth, her fire, mourned their loss. Teachers, students, mothers, daughters — all products of Rebbetzin Kaplan's work — felt the emptiness, the darkness. Yet, although we no longer have the actual flame, the rays still reach us, guide us and show us the way.

Dear Rebbetzin Kaplan,

You are probably very surprised that I did not register for the new term. Of course I know that we have over one hundred girls in Bais Yaakov so you surely do not even know who I am. But I know who you are and I think of you every day. And that is why I am writing you about my problem.

My parents won't let me come back to Bais Yaakov. They think I am too religious and they have already registered me in the high school there. How can I go to public school after being here in Bais Yaakov for a year?

Every day I fight with my mother. I know the holy Torah says I'm not allowed to, but what can I do? How can I live without Bais Yaakov? How can I make my family understand that Bais Yaakov is my life?

Please don't answer my letter because my parents will be angry if they find out that I wrote to you but I had to tell you what is in my heart. I want to tell you, dear Rebbetzin Kaplan, that I will, *im yirtzeh Hashem*, be back in Bais Yaakov. I don't know how, but I'm sure *Hashem* will help me to continue in Bais Yaakov — I have *bitachon* that He will help me.

A Loving Bais Yaakov Girl Forever

This letter was written to Rebbetzin Kaplan in the early 1950's.